HOUSING HEAVEN'S FIRE

The Challenge of Holiness

JOHN C. HAUGHEY, S.J.

an imprint of
LOYOLAPRESS.
CHICAGO

an imprint of

LOYOLAPRESS.

3441 N. ASHLAND AVENUE
CHICAGO, ILLINOIS 60657

Library of Congress Cataloging-in-Publication Data

Haughey, John C.
   Housing heaven's fire : the challenge of holiness / John C. Haughey.
     p. cm.
   Includes bibliographical references.
   ISBN 0-8294-1469-X
    1. Holiness.   I. Title

BT767 .H37 2002
234'.8—dc21

                             2002067107

Printed in the United States of America

  3 4 5 6 7 8 9 Versa 9 8 7 6 5 4 3

Contents

Introduction

MY FIELD OF STUDY IS ETHICS, more precisely, Christian ethics. Much as I have admired this discipline and learned from it, I have always been disappointed that most of its authors have failed to address one topic, the topic of holiness. The way the ancients addressed the discipline of ethics was through accounts of what constituted "the good." Plato flirted with the idea of the holy but couldn't get very far with it. Christian ethicists have no such excuse since the good graduates into the holy in their faith. Isn't the good an unfinished masterpiece until it is crowned with or crests with the holy? The good floats off into a myriad of conflicted understandings if it has no place to go but sideways and around and around.

This book wants to fill in some of the lacuna about the good by relating it to holiness. Its method will be to engage the scriptural and doctrinal texts that focus the mind on the subject. Although the work is an exercise in theological reflection, I do not engage many theologians and ethicists since there are few who have addressed the subject. My style will be appreciative and meditative rather than argumentative or exhortative.

A few words about fire. Untamed, fire has always been a catastrophe. It wasn't until humans could tame fire for purposes such as cooking, forging metals, lighting the darkness, and warming themselves that civilization began. At one point in humans' connection with fire a marvel presented itself: a bush that was burning but was not consumed (Exod. 3:2). This is the start of something big, Moses realized—benign fire. A new level of civilization was about to begin. Soon we have the pillar of fire guiding the Israelites out of slavery toward the land flowing with milk and honey. Skip a while and we have the undying lamp in the temple representing Yahweh's undying presence to Israel. For the Israelites, fire had a theocentric rather than a cosmological ring to it. The coming of Jesus did not change this. John the Baptist heralded one difference: the fire would be within. Jesus would baptize with the Holy Spirit and with fire (Luke 3:16). Indeed, Jesus confirmed that he came to light a fire on earth and was impatient for the blaze to be ignited (Luke 12:49). And, sure enough, with Pentecost, tongues of fire appeared on those on whom the Spirit came to rest. So, God's holiness is well described by the symbol fire.

The purpose of the book is to enchant the reader with the fact and fire of holiness. When I was young, holiness enchanted me. It didn't seem preposterous to aspire to it then. Children have great appetites for dreaming up larger-than-life scenarios within which they can imagine themselves playing the role their fantasy fuels. But their immediate culture must feed and reinforce this aspiration. Mine did. The saints were real to my family, with the Mother of all saints the most real of these haloed figures. Gradually, however, I became disenchanted with the aspiration about holiness. This was partly due to a change of venue—when I was thirteen my family moved from a small town to a large city, where "church" became much more impersonal and nature was intercepted by a paved-over world where work was central and relationships functional. The disenchantment was also due to changes in me—holiness became a merely moral matter in a moralistic environment, or so it seems to me looking back on it.

Sociologists, psychologists, anthropologists, and educators would all have much to say about this process of disenchantment. They would tell us that it is an inevitable phase of child development and a very real part of our culture. I am certainly prepared to concede that disenchantment is an essential part of personal and human evolution. However, it has a frequently overlooked cost as well. When we have become disenchanted, we see the ordinary as reality and easily become absorbed in the everyday and resigned to the mundane. In this limited worldview, our aspirations shrink. Should I—should we—settle for the small, here-and-now aspirations and forget that there is something beyond what we can see that is in fact still attainable? Do we, the members of the church, really aspire to this beyond, this holiness?

This book is not an exercise in nostalgia that tries to get back to a childish understanding of holiness. It accepts the disenchantment and will seek to re-enchant it. We don't have to remain in the state of disenchantment, nor should we grow exhausted pursuing small aspirations. It's poison to settle for less than we were scripted to be. The only medium available to me is words. The words I will use to re-enchant holiness in this book are meant to reach the mind of the reader. Whether they will reach the heart and "stir into flame the gift of God" (2 Tim. 1:6) once bestowed on you is not within my power to effect.

A brief description of the seven chapters. The first is in awe of the fact that holiness is not an achievement we are capable of. Nor should it be. Showing how it is an *already* not a *not-yet* kind of thing takes it out of the realm of something to be achieved. The second chapter brings us into the story of holiness in order to appreciate it in the rich diversity with which it has been presented in the Hebrew Scriptures. The childlike Israel appropriated these stories. Holiness, since it cannot be contained within a concept, is closer to intelligibility *via* story. The third chapter is somewhat of an irony. I felt the need to disenchant notions about Jesus' holiness in order to take the best icon we have for holiness and make him more available to us in a way often overlooked in Christological study. The fourth chapter addresses the question of our desires and where holiness resides within them. The fifth chapter gets more specific and appreciates St. Paul's metaphor of stretching, which makes it clear that the glory of God, not growth in our own holiness, is the desire the Spirit stirs up in the believer. In the sixth chapter holiness gets legs, so to speak, and walks out into society. It is concerned with the idea of solidarity and how solidarity is God's holy agenda. The final chapter connects this move toward solidarity with the insights into human rights that have to become central to the mission of Christ and his church in society for the rest of history.

A book is delivered with the help of midwives. Three have been especially helpful at critical moments in this birthing process, Ginny Novak, Terri MacKenzie, S.H.C.J., and Mary Lane. It goes through different trimesters. The first of these was endured by students at John Carroll University during the year I held the Touhy Chair. The second was suffered by students at the Summer Institute at Spring Hill. Three people were especially helpful at this stage of gestation: Dan Hartnett, Bliss Browne, and Dick Luecke. By the time the third trimester arrived, my dear and very unpretentious prayer group (which goes by the pretentious name of the Community of His Kingdom) could hear the heartbeats. The whole process was assisted by my Jesuit colleagues in the theology department at Loyola University Chicago and the graduate students who are such a delight to work with.

1

Receiving the Gift

I SUPPOSE I ALWAYS SAW HOLINESS as something good, though rare. It was aspired to by few and realized by even fewer. After my young years, I myself did not aspire to it or even think much about it. For me, "being real" usually felt like a better aspiration and one I was closer to attaining. And, like most people I know, "just keeping it together" was as good an aim as I could muster.

In the last few years, for reasons I don't fully understand, holiness has increasingly become an aspiration of mine. Not knowing exactly why holiness began to attract me anew, I began to ask others about their attitudes toward it. My informal surveying included students in several graduate and undergraduate classes I have taught. The most memorable reply was that of a ponytailed sophomore who seemed incapable of smiling. She said she was totally turned off by the very idea of holiness. To her it smacked of hypocrisy or even of religious fanaticism. But she was the exception. Some of the students in the same class expressed an attraction to it, with a few of them saying they aspired to it. Most, however, hadn't thought about it, had never

talked about it, and couldn't even recall a conversation in which
the topic was broached. By far the most interesting reaction
came from another class, where a priest student answered that
he considered aspiring to holiness to be "Promethean." He was
referring to the Titan of Greek mythology who stole fire from
heaven and whom angry Zeus lashed to a mountain. His comment stopped me in my tracks. Were my interest in and desire
for holiness a vain, presumptuous, unrealistic effort to steal fire
from heaven? This book is an effort to answer no to this question. It will seek to establish that the fire is neither stolen nor is
it absent from us earthlings.

In this chapter I would like to stimulate my readers to desire
to take an inventory of their own views on this subject. Is the desire
for holiness a Promethean lurch away from our earthly condition?
Since I don't believe it is, I will present a few of the ideas on holiness that have deepened my attraction to it, though my attraction
came before I could say exactly why I was enchanted by it.

For starters, aspiring to holiness is a way of living one's
life. It is a way of seeing our lives, my own or another's, and of
thinking about our purposes. It is more than thinking about
who I am. It entails a choosing of who I want to become on the
basis of what I see holiness to be. It must also contend with contrary emotional states—deciding what to make of them and do
with them, especially when they are blue or dark or shamefully
un-Promethean and very far from feeling holy or even caring
about it. Holiness also has something to do with morality; morality must be part of the content of holiness, even if the connection remains somewhat obscure.

Vatican II spent some time on the subject of holiness, underscoring that it is a call. But a call from whom? Whose calling? And
what is the call to? The council addresses these questions in *Lumen*

Gentium (LG). It is a call from God. It is a call to be holy just as the Father, Son, and Spirit are holy. It is a call to be "perfect, just as your heavenly Father is perfect" (Matt. 5:48). The council describes God as "the Author and Finisher of this holiness of life." And it is to that end that the Holy Spirit is sent: "To inspire us from within to love God with our whole heart, soul, mind, and strength." The call is "to the fullness of the Christian life and the perfection of charity" (*LG*, 39).[1] Jesus is then described as "the model of all perfection."

So the author of the aspiration to holiness is the Spirit, and the call is to be holy after the manner of the Trinity itself. If the Spirit is putting this aspiration into your heart, you aren't stealing fire from heaven—it is being bestowed. It is a gift to be received and cherished. And the measure of our holiness will be Jesus—his love of God and of others. Jesus' holiness and ours come from the same source.

Since this can all seem terribly lofty, I want to emphasize one surprising comment that the council makes. It describes holiness as "a *more human* way of life."[2] It would be quite an accomplishment for the future direction of human history if we could show that holiness is a more human way of life than any other way of living or aspiring to live. If "holy" is not the opposite of being human but the *more human* way to be, that would surely be news! I will not succeed in establishing this beyond any doubt, but I will attempt to make a good case for it.

Obviously, the council did not concoct this idea of a call to holiness out of its own imagination. The call had been heard and recorded in Christian hearts from the beginning. Thus, Paul assured the Ephesians that "the God and Father of our Lord Jesus Christ . . . chose us in him, before the foundation of the world, to be holy and without blemish before him [in love]" (Eph. 1:3–4). Nor, of course, was it original with Paul. Israel had heard the same call, as we will spell out in the next chapter. Pointedly, one thinks of Leviticus 19:2: "Be holy, for I, the LORD, your God, am holy."

Also intriguing is the council's judgment that the holiness we all are called to is the same holiness: "One and the same holiness are cultivated by all who are moved by the Spirit of God" (*LG*, 41). Maybe this should not be all that surprising, since God is one and God alone is holy. But Catholics have to overcome a deep bias to accept the fact that it is the same holiness we are all called to. This bias is that some—for instance, religious or priests, bishops or popes—are called to a different holiness than everyone else. This bias has probably been reinforced by the fact that most of the canonized saints were popes, bishops, priests, and religious. They were and still are considered the professionally holy ones, whereas the rest of us amateurs just barely get by.

But the proof of the sameness of the holiness to which all are called is traceable to a single historical moment and to the singular act that was performed at that moment. "By this 'will' [God's], we have been [sanctified] through the offering of the body of Jesus Christ. . . . By one offering he has made perfect forever those who are being [sanctified]" (Heb. 10:10, 14). This stunning truth, that the redeeming act of Christ "perfected for all time those who are being sanctified," sits largely unnoticed at the center of our Christian faith. And who are these sanctified? Those who believe in the Christ. But how many of those who do believe in the Christ believe that this offering, which was made "once and for all," has perfected them and sanctifies them?[3]

In this view of holiness, however, there seem to be two conflicting ideas. Are we *already* "perfected/sanctified/consecrated," or are we called to become such? The council's formula suggests both: we are to "hold on to and complete in our lives that sanctification which we have received" (*LG*, 40). This exhortation of the council is, in effect, to "become the saints you already are." Or as Peter puts it,

"Be holy yourselves in every aspect of your conduct, for it is written, 'Be holy because I [am] holy'" (1 Pet. 1:15–16).

Not an Achievement

The most difficult issue in this whole matter of holiness and call is understanding that the holiness we are called to has already been received. But if it has already happened, what is the call to? It is a call to own our own holiness, to take as having been done unto me and to us what happened centuries before there was a me and an us. What is to be owned is that we have already been made holy. "The temple of God, which you are, is holy" (1 Cor. 3:17). If this is so, then holiness is not something we must achieve, a mountain we have still to scale. Rather, it is to be awakened to as already a reality, already true and operative. Nor is this received holiness static. It is God continuing to act in us toward an end not yet in sight. "I am confident of this, that the one who began a good work in you will continue to complete it until the day of Christ Jesus" (Phil. 1:6). We are a holy work still in progress. To know this is the beginning of the re-enchantment of holiness.

What would change if I sat myself down and arrived at the deep conviction that I am holy—already? It seems to me much would change. For starters, in my sense of self there would be a self-acceptance, even an awe about what I have been made. There would be peace, because so much of what I have been striving to become I am already. I would spend time in the simple appreciation of what has already been "done unto me"! If one is already a temple of God, then the temple doesn't have to be built by human hands or strivings. A self that is housing the holiness of God is a self that can afford to have a deep self-love built on the rock of truth. One doesn't have to wait for today's kudos and tomorrow's applause, which either never come or never come thunderously enough. Aspirations about holiness must begin with appreciation of and thankfulness for what is already so.

The second change would be in how I would view members of my family, my friends, colleagues, neighbors, even my enemies—in a word, the other. If I had this conviction, I would act as though the other was a sanctuary that housed the awesome presence of the Holy God. In the presence of the Holy, wouldn't it be right at the very least to take off one's shoes and proceed inside—frequently and with a sense of deep reverence, hoping for encounter? Granted, not every human edifice houses the holiness of God, but all have been built to do so. Whether a person is rejecting or accepting this gift is usually beyond our ability to judge. What we can judge, however, is the intention of God to dwell in holiness in what has already been made in God's own image and likeness.

The third change would be in how we view God. With the Beyond already within, why would there not be a prayerful, ongoing dialogue with this Beyond? Or, at least, an exquisite care about the treasure we carry and are carried by? A helpful analogue might be imagining Mary's nine-month pregnancy, what she carried and how she carried herself. Or think of Isaiah when he was overtaken by a vision of "the Lord seated on a high and lofty throne, with the train of his garment filling the temple," with the seraphim crying out to one another, "Holy, holy, holy is the LORD of hosts" (Isa. 6:1–3). It is the beginning of wisdom to be awed by God and the beginning of an appropriate response to God's holiness to thank and praise God for not withholding it from us. Or if that is too steep a climb from where you are standing right now, think of the awe and exuberance that accompanied "the real presence" housed in the ark of the covenant. "Happy the people who know you LORD, who walk in the radiance of your face" (Ps. 89:16).

A Receivement

Holiness, therefore, has been misconstrued. We've come to see it as something other than what has been revealed. In our ignorance we see it as something that we have to perform ourselves into. This is why it is left to others. But holiness as performance is simply not true! Holiness is being done unto us, not by us. And since it has already begun, we don't act in order to come into the condition of holiness; we act from within its unmerited but already-in-place reality.

Before we respond with pious activity, we should contemplate the divine accomplishment of Jesus Christ. Once we begin to comprehend the good news about holiness, our actions will give evidence of it, and the disappointment with ourselves as wanting in it can be dismissed as ignorance that we have already gained access to the inner life of the Holy One.

The fact of having received the gift of holiness by clinging to the fact of Christ's death on our behalf denies that we still have a long way to go. But as works in progress, acts of repentance are never inappropriate. Being *simul justus et peccator* (righteous and sinful persons simultaneously), we are never wholly holy in this life. Repentance is never out of place, but it can become a form of works-righteousness if we make more of repentance for sin than of acts of gratitude and praise for the "righteousness" that has been won for us at the cost of Jesus' own life. A consciousness of sin can develop that doesn't even suspect the need for a consciousness of holiness. We are meant to live in the joy that we've been redeemed, not in the pain of a redemption that is beyond our reach.

A Work in Progress

Holiness looked at experientially is a subtle issue. Do I, John Haughey, experience myself as holy? Not really! Am I, in fact? Yes! But if that is so, what to make of the nearly universal experience of the saints? It seems that the more they experienced God's holiness and were drawn into that holiness, the more aware they were of the contrast between God's infinite holiness and their being wanting in it. In this they seem to have been like Peter. Recall his protestation: "Depart from me, Lord, for I am a sinful man," which erupted at the moment he saw Jesus' power over nature. Because Jesus knew where the fish of the sea were, this hapless fisherman could let down his nets and be overwhelmed by the catch. This is a seeming contradiction— the closer one is to God, the more aware one is of one's unholiness. The more of God we know, the greater becomes our capacity for God. We are *capax infiniti,* born with a limitless capacity for the limitless God. So, the closer we are drawn into the holiness of God, the greater is our capacity for God. This paradox is similar to having an insatiable thirst for God while at the same time experiencing the "rivers of living water [that] will flow from within [them]" (John 7:38).

The Letter to the Hebrews

We need to go back to the text from Hebrews because to do so will help us to skewer several other strong, culturally reinforced biases that prevent us from hearing the call to holiness. One of these is a repugnance for the pious. Being "pious" suggests being so nice that one is out of touch with oneself, or self-deceived, or maybe even a phony. Another bias is that holiness is unrealistic, insufficiently hard-nosed, or escapist. Still another of these biases is that I would take holiness seriously if it were an essential of the faith, but it mustn't be since it doesn't seem to be preached or spoken of explicitly by ordinary believers. Therefore, the bias would say, it must belong to the optional world of "heroic" behavior like poverty, chastity, and obedience. The final and most pervasive of these biases is that holiness is too remote. My life is so busy; I have enough on my plate already. So I surely don't have time to give attention to something as far away from me as holiness, since I'm barely keeping it together as it is.

The antidote to bias is knowledge and understanding. Here I want to expand our knowledge about holiness by delving deeper into the already mentioned letter to the Hebrews. It overturns the biases listed above. This letter is a "message of encouragement" (Heb. 13:22) about the sanctification of believers. It isn't an easy read because it presumes that the reader has some background knowledge of Old Testament cultic purifications and types of sacrifice. The author's main insight in this letter is that Jesus subsumed the Jewish sacrificial system into himself by his obedience to the intention God had in mandating Israel's sacrifices in the first place. Israel's purpose in performing its cultic rituals was for the worshipers to grow more one with God and God's will for them. But in the fullness of time, one of these worshipers fully succeeded in doing this. Jesus of Nazareth, as the Hebrews text puts it, committed himself to do what God had intended for Israel to do: God's will! "I come to do your will, O God" (Heb. 10:7).

This one act of Jesus' wholly obedient will, made in time by this one man, changed everything for the future of the world, for history, for civilization, and, finally, for me and you, completely. "By this 'will,' we have been consecrated through the offering of the body of Jesus Christ [his self offering] once for all" (Heb. 10:10). Everything Israel's history of cultic sacrifice and ritual purification was meant to accomplish has now been accomplished by and in him. Jesus' followers must know what was effected by his offering of himself on the cross, namely, that "by one offering he has made perfect forever those who are being consecrated" (Heb. 10:14).

This one line should eradicate the bias that holiness is a peripheral matter or a pious option one can make if he or she feels up to it. And it should skewer the bias that holiness is a work to be accomplished, something above and beyond the call of duty, something one might get around to if one felt so inclined and had no other agenda. In fact, it would not be seen as a *work* at all. It requires all believers to stop giving mere lip service to the belief that Christ died for our sins, recognizing the truth of the amazing claim that "he has made perfect forever those who are being consecrated." In the new covenant, the frequent repetitions of "those same sacrifices that can never take away sins," have been superseded by Jesus, who "offered one sacrifice for sins, and took his seat forever at the right hand of God" (Heb. 10:11–12).

The difference between the old covenant and the new has never been so clearly articulated. The author insists that "the holy Spirit testifies" that "there is no longer offering for sin" (Heb. 10:15, 18). If we misconstrue the meaning of this once-and-for-all act of Jesus' self-offering, the text warns that a punishment will ensue (Heb. 10:29). I interpret this not as a punishment to be inflicted by God but the punishment we inflict on ourselves for looking past the radical transformation this redeeming act of Christ has already brought about in us. Our punishment, then, will consist in having the unrelieved itch of thinking our salvation is something we have still to bring about ourselves, like a work to be accomplished by our wills, or a mountain we still have to climb if and when we get around to it.

We need, therefore, to ponder these words: "He has perfected forever those who are being sanctified." Who are these people, and how are they being sanctified? In one sense, everyone has been redeemed by the blood of Christ.[4] But objective redemption awaits its subjective reception. For Christians, this reception is through belief, and appropriation is signified by their baptism. For all other peoples, whose faith is not known to us, how this objective redemption touches them is something only God can know.

I find it interesting that the verb the author of Hebrews uses here is not a past but a present participle—*hagiazomenous*—"being sanctified." This indicates that sanctification is a work in progress. Although this is the work of all three divine Persons, it is to God the Father that the initiation of the work is attributed, and our being sanctified is attributed to the Spirit, while having been perfected is attributed to Christ. It would seem, therefore, that there are two parts, or moments, of God's work in us.[5] Passivity is not the right response to this work in progress, of course. Rather, both the active belief and the subsequent discipline of participation in this truth are needed to awaken us more and more to what has been and is continuing to be done unto us even now.

One of the great values of Eucharist is its power to enable us to participate in the truth of the event that has been our salvation. It is the occasion for an ever deeper appreciation of this still hard-to-believe good news. Eucharist is not a sin offering to God who is patiently awaiting people to become purified through their ritual performances. It is the act that celebrates our being consecrated and set apart. Again and again, it evokes our yes to what has been done on our behalf by God. At its deepest meaning, Eucharist is an

act of thanksgiving for what we have already received, the sanctifying effects of which are still reverberating within us.

The author of this Hebrews letter invites the reader to
delight in a relationship with God that is infinitely more secure
than the old covenant relationship. As the letter puts it, ours is a
"better covenant" with "better promises" and a "better hope" than
Israel could ever have imagined. This optimism rests on the present perfect tense of the verb used here—*teteleiōken*—"he has
made perfect [for all time]"; it's a done deal! Our ongoing sanctification is "part of the process of eschatological perfection
achieved through the perfecting of Christ" (Heb. 2:10; 5:9; 7:28)
(Ibid., 37). This is not an invitation to be presumptuous, since we
can always fall away from faith. If we were to import the thought
of Paul into the optimism of the letter to the Hebrews, he would
assure us that we can presume that the One who began this good
work in us will complete it (if we let God have "his" way) on the
day of the Lord Jesus (Phil. 1:6). In brief, then, since he has "forever perfected those who are being sanctified," a past act is continuing to invite us to grow in God even as I write and you read.
The letter to the Hebrews reminds us of the dynamism of holiness
and keeps us from seeing it as out of reach and a static ideal for
those who might have the time or the energy for it.

A Deeper Cleansing

We should emphasize one further understanding of the author of
the letter to the Hebrews about the act of purification. In the Old
Testament "the blood of goats and bulls and the sprinkling of a
heifer's ashes" were used to overcome defilement. The result was that
supposedly the worshipers' "flesh is cleansed" (Heb. 9:13). The desire

to be holy in God's sight led Israel to perform innumerable cleansing rituals—some personal, such as washing one's hands, some cultic, such as the bloody sacrifices alluded to here. But if one were to be cleansed with the blood of Christ, what would be washed then? Not the outward but the innermost part of a person, which is the heart and the conscience. For if the flesh (in the sense of that which is out of touch with God) is cleansed by the blood of sacrificed animals, "how much more will the blood of Christ, who through the eternal spirit offered himself unblemished to God, cleanse our consciences from dead works to worship the living God?" (Heb. 9:14).

In temple worship "gifts and sacrifices are offered that cannot perfect the worshiper in conscience" (Heb. 9:9). Consequently, within Israel's self-understanding there remained a residue of guilt or a burdened conscience. But Jesus has created a better covenant because the conscience has been made clean; the heart of a person has been washed in the blood of the Lamb so that the law could now be in the heart. This was what the prophecies of Jeremiah 31–33 and Ezekiel 36:26–27 had implied, namely, that in the new dispensation God's law would be placed in the heart. The Law was holy for Israel as it is for the new Israel, but it is now located in a new place, the heart cleansed with the blood of Christ. Christ's sacrifice is the answer to Israel's prayer: "A clean heart create for me, God;/renew in me a steadfast spirit" (Ps. 51:12).

As an aside: Hebrews has often been interpreted as supporting anti-Semitism. Paul's letter to the Romans is a better reminder that Israel remains holy in the eyes of God. "If the firstfruits are holy, so is the whole batch of dough; and if the root is holy, so are the branches" (Rom. 11:16). The first fruits and the root are both Israel. Even more pointed is Paul's remark that "in respect to election, they [the Jews] are beloved [by God] because of the patriarchs. For the gifts and the call of God are irrevocable" (Rom. 11:28–29). Norbert Lohfink has cogently argued that there has been only one covenant and that it has never been revoked.[6] This is surely good news!

Covered Over with Concepts

I believe holiness lost its enchantment in the church because historically there has been an inadequate elaboration of the subject. If we were to be complete in our analysis, we would have to go back to the creation story and see there how God meant humanity to be in union with God and to that end supplied Adam and Eve with "original justice," as the Catholic tradition prefers to call it. But it seems to me that, more proximately, two categories of the Catholic tradition, grace and justification, have absorbed too much attention and analysis, to the detriment of the category of holiness. Grace could have enchanted us if the favor or graciousness of God toward us had been kept front and center. Instead, complex scholastic disquisitions on grace with their many subtle distinctions and subdivisions have overwhelmed the simple message of God's reaching out to us with God's own Self. The beauty of the forest is lost when each tree is singled out, dissected, reified, and analyzed in isolation from the whole. The root meaning of grace is that God's favor or graciousness is being showered upon us completely.

But even more disenchanting, at least for me, has been the degree of emphasis placed on "justification" since Luther and the Council of Trent (1545–1563). Neither of these treatments, either of grace or of justification, was or is in error, of course, but the terminology, the analysis, and the history of the wrangling over these can easily rob the Christ-event of its simple power and beauty. We land on the concepts, and the event from which they were conceived becomes obscured. It was inevitable, I suppose, that Paul would make a big issue of justification/righteousness as his central insight into the Christ-event because of his own spiritual upbringing and training. He was not unfamiliar with other ways of understanding the Christ-event, such as salvation, new creation, expiation, freedom, forgiveness of sins, liberation, reconciliation, and sanctification. Though all these terms were understood and used by him, his main focus was on justification.

The Council of Trent's decree on justification addressed the Lutheran emphasis on justification but unfortunately became riveted to Luther's questions and issues. The beauty of the deed Christ has done for us and unto us gets lost in terminological squabbles about works and justification, which too easily led us to focus on ourselves rather than on the praise that should be offered for the deed done on our behalf. Our "proper" moral response to the deed becomes more important than the personal relationship with God that the Christ-event makes possible. Lost, too, is our spontaneous response of gratitude and love for these gifts. We have minimized the real, interpersonal relations with each of the divine Persons that creation and the Christ-event enable us to have. Granted, the redeeming act of Christ has made us right with God, or if you will, it has justified us. But it has justified us in order for us to participate as persons in the life the three divine Persons have with one another. Rather than focus all our attention on justification, I believe we need to appreciate the call to enjoy and glory in the triune relations available to us in the Spirit.

The Spirit's Role

The underdevelopment of the theology of the Holy Spirit (pneumatology) in the West is one of the main culprits behind our spiritual impoverishment. It is the Spirit who makes possible the several unities we need to be a holy people. These unities are between ourselves and each of the divine Persons as well as our unities with one another. The Spirit, furthermore, brings the past (and the cross) into the present (and the worshipful, grateful celebration of the believing community) so that the already-begun eschatological glory (holiness) grows in the hearts of believers. The main unity the Spirit assists us with is, of course, love of the God who first loved us. The Spirit even enables us to love a future we do not see and vectors us toward it. Because of the Spirit we can fulfill the hope expressed by Christ in his Last Supper discourse that his followers would abide in his love (John 15:9). Abiding in his love with the help of the Spirit can be lost as an overriding purpose when there is an arid doctrinalizing of the Christ-event or an overconceptualism of categories (such as grace or justification), abstracted from the love that has reached out to bring us into God's own love life.

Greater attention to the movements within us of the Spirit should help us sense that there is a drama going on right beneath the surface of our ordinary lives. By gentle nudges God, through the Spirit's gifts, would draw us into a conflation between all that touches our lives and the mystery of Christ (Eph. 1:10). To know that this is the direction of what God is drawing us to requires the gift of the Spirit. As Paul tells us, "No one knows what pertains to God except the Spirit of God" (1 Cor. 2:11). The purpose of the cross was that we might receive the Spirit (Gal. 3:13–14). Why has the Spirit been conferred on us? Among other things, so that we could know "the thoughts of God."

Any knowledge we have of God not only comes from but also is knowledge of the Spirit. For Paul, to be in Christ meant that we could live by and be led by the Spirit (Gal. 5:16–18). Because of Christ we can live our lives by "the law of the spirit" (Rom. 8:2) and have the mind of the Spirit.

The Spirit was not simply an idea for Paul or for his communities but an unforgettable experience (Gal. 3:2; Rom. 3:24; 2 Cor. 6:1). Though "one can reflect theologically in the Holy Spirit, [one cannot reflect] on the Holy Spirit as an entity," as Kilian McDonnell puts it. He observes that the Spirit is more like the total horizon within which we know God, and "not a specialized object within the horizon nor a section of the vista."[7] So in the mind of the author of Hebrews, it was "through the eternal spirit [that Christ] offered himself unblemished to God, [so that the blood of Christ could] cleanse our consciences from dead works to worship the living God" (Heb. 9:14). There are two dependencies on the Holy Spirit implied here, that of Christ's humanity and of our own. Everything I believe I know about the Christ-event relies on this same Spirit—to make manifest to us the incomparable wealth we have in the cross of Christ, as well as our call to live, as those who have been raised up to live, a life free from dead works, especially the dead work of trying to make ourselves holy.

Human holiness has evolved: creation, exodus, Sinai, the prophets, the return from Babylon, the incarnation when the Spirit came upon Mary and overshadowed her (Luke 1:35), Jesus' anointing at the river Jordan when "the holy Spirit descended upon him in bodily form like a dove" (Luke 3:22), and on the cross when he handed over his spirit (John 19:30). Once the alabaster jar of Jesus' own humanity was broken at his death, the whole house of the world could be perfumed by the Spirit. Where the perfume of the Spirit is, there is love, joy, peace, patience, kindness, generosity, faithfulness, gentleness, and self-control. These are the fragrant fruits of the Spirit.[8]

The ontologizing mind, which thinks in terms of natures and essences, likes to begin with the incarnation to understand the mystery of Christ. The historical mind, which is the mind of most of us, prefers a more functional way of understanding Jesus. So we start with his being anointed at his baptism. What best explains the people of God to themselves is their being anointed by God by sharing in Christ's anointing with the Spirit. As Augustine expressed it: "We are all the body of Christ because we all share in the anointing and, in him, we are all Christ's and Christ, since in a certain way the whole Christ consists in both Head and Body." Or, as Cyril of Jerusalem expresses it:

> "As partakers of Christ you are rightly called Christs, that is, anointed ones." Heribert Muehlen's way of understanding this anointing is to say that the church is not a prolongation of Christ's human body, that is to say of the incarnation, but it is in the strict sense a prolongation of the Spirit of Christ, of his anointing and of his grace, his *gratia capitis* (the grace of the head), and the unique and incommunicable holiness he has as only begotten son of God made flesh. (Cantalamessa, 16)

The New Way of Being Perfect (Matthew 5:48)

If we have already been perfected, as Paul claims, why would Jesus have exhorted his listeners to "be perfect, just as your heavenly Father is perfect"? (Matt. 5:48). Was their perfection their work? The context of the Sermon on the Mount must be examined to answer this. Jesus had informed his listeners that his disciples' perfection had to exceed that of the scribes and Pharisees. He also informed them that he came to fulfill the law rather than to abolish it (Matt. 5:17). He then proceeded to inform them how their righteousness could exceed the more externally measurable righteousness of the law's observance (Matt. 5:18-20). His criteria, or norms, for their perfection were interior. So, for example, they were to go beyond obeying the prohibition against murder and adultery by not allowing their hearts to nurse any grudges of anger, nor was there to be the slightest yielding of their hearts to lust (Matt. 5:21–28).

The whole Sermon on the Mount is, according to both Augustine and Thomas Aquinas, an elaboration about what is new about the new law.[9] Its normativity does not consist in new oughts and ought nots. It centers righteousness not in behavior but in the heart, where Jesus' was. His interiority was the center for his obedience to the God he came to understand. He does not introduce new practices but rather new attitudes. Jesus wants his followers' dispositions to be like his and, therefore, like God's. So, for example, rather than love just some, those who are nice to you, love those who are hostile to you. Be centers not of retribution but of a love that is willing to be unilateral. Go beyond the iron law of reciprocity in your behavior with one another. Generate love for others without calculating "what's in it for me." In this way they would become "perfect, just as your heavenly Father is perfect" (Matt. 5:48).

Matthew's new understanding of perfection was in contrast to the Greek, or Stoic, understanding as well as to the rabbinic understanding. According to the Greek model, virtues must be developed by strength of will and good character. This Greek/Stoic version of perfection had the eye fixed on the self. By contrast, the rabbinic version had the eye fixed on the law. Rabbinic Judaism, which arose after the fall of the temple in 70 C.E., was probably the main competition contending for the allegiance of Matthew's audience. It had been adamant about the particulars of the law, believing that they must be exactly observed. The new law of Jesus had the eye fixed on God, to whom Jesus prayed and bore witness and ultimately, at whose behest he died. Jesus' followers were to be baptized in the name of Father, Son, and Spirit (Matt. 28:19).

Baptism lodged the desire for perfection not primarily in the will, as with the Stoics, nor in the law, as with the Jews, but in the heart. It would be a while, in fact centuries, before a Trinitarian doctrine would be fully articulated in the church, since the Trinitarian character of God was only beginning to be understood at the time of the Gospels. When the doctrine matured, it would be clear that the Spirit indwelling the heart would be the new center from which the perfection of the Christian would take its inspiration. Like Jesus, the followers of Jesus would act on what the Spirit taught them, in their hearts, was the mind of God as it came to be known through its embodiment in the words and deeds and life of the Son of God.

The consoling points, therefore, are, first, that we are being made perfect/holy; we do not make ourselves perfect/holy. Second, the energy for living a holy life is already available to us. Third, we can know the particulars entailed in living this way of life by attention to the Spirit indwelling us. Fourth, that the "perfection" that we will eventually attain is that which humanly and distinctively replicates the perfection of God as we know that from Christ.

The Holiness of the Church

Paul had the interesting habit of canonizing whole communities by calling them the saints even when he was quite clear that they were in error about some important aspect of the faith. To correct them is why he wrote most of the letters he did. He wasn't contradicting himself by calling them saints, since in faith they adhered to the Holy One of God. These communities were each as a bride that the bridegroom had chosen to be wedded to. "I betrothed you to one husband to present you as a chaste virgin to Christ" (2 Cor. 11:2). He could say this even though he knew a given community had been blindsided by "a different gospel" and had lost their doctrinal purity by subscribing to these deviant versions of the faith (2 Cor. 11:3–4). Paul saw his own function as ensuring that the bride with the blemish became chaste not in the moral sense but by coming to the knowledge of the truth the community had in Christ Jesus.

So Paul never uses the term *saint* in the singular, choosing instead to address always "the saints," for example, "to you who have been sanctified in Christ Jesus, called to be holy [saints together]" (1 Cor. 1:2). What is behind his great reserve about predicating sanctity of an individual is his realization that it is the whole community of the faithful who are made holy by Christ's redeeming act and are called to live as one in that holiness. And insofar as they do, God's plan is being carried out. That plan: "In [Christ Jesus] you also are being built together into a dwelling place of God in the Spirit" (Eph. 2:22).

But a further consideration is that no canonized saint has become a saint independently of the communities within which they lived and moved and had their being. It is the community of faith that articulates the Gospel and provides the place for the individual's response to it. Especially with its eucharistic celebrations, the holiness of God renews the community and the individuals in it. The body of Christ is just this: members mediating the holiness of God to members and, through the unity the Spirit gives through this, cohering to one another in a communion with God. At least that is what God would effect, presuming we allow it. While God has a personal relationship with each of us, this relationship comes through the community of those who are in Christ. "It has pleased God to make men holy and save them not merely as individuals, without any mutual bonds, but by making them into a single people, a people which acknowledges Him in truth and serves Him in holiness." It is our solidarity with one another in faith, hope, and love that offers "flawless glory to God" (Vatican II *Gaudium et Spes* [GS], 32).

We have to ground personal holiness in something deeper than the individual. Individually holy persons would be too thin a reed to carry the weight being placed on the theme of this volume. Should the church be seen as the locus of personal holiness? Is it substantially holy? The Second Vatican Council would say yes to both these questions. Its holiness is so substantial that it "can never fail" (*LG*, 39). The church is holy because God has chosen to make the church "the temple of the Holy Spirit" (*LG*, 17). This holiness has its origin and cause in the fact that Christ "loved the Church as his bride, delivering himself up for her. He did this that he might sanctify her" (*LG*, 39). Furthermore, "he united himself to her as his own body and crowned her with the gift of the Holy Spirit for the glory of God" (*LG*, 39).

This has been the church's self-understanding from the beginning. In the New Testament we can find: "You also are being built together into a dwelling place of God in the Spirit" (Eph. 2:22). The creeds affirm this: "I believe in one, *holy*, catholic and apostolic Church." As the Second Vatican Council suggestively puts it, the Holy Spirit was sent on the day of Pentecost "to continually sanctify [the church]" (*LG*, 4). The presence in the church of this continuously sanctifying Spirit, who "vivifies, unifies, and moves the whole body," is what makes this mystery of the church's holiness a reality. "In order that we may be unceasingly renewed in him, he [Christ] has shared with us his Spirit who, existing as one and the same being in the head and in the members, vivifies, unifies, and moves the whole body" (*LG*, 7). If all of this seems less than obvious about the church, whose sinfulness is regularly covered in the secular media, the council would concede that we know about the holiness of the church only in a "shadowed way until at the last it will be revealed in total splendor" (*LG*, 8).

So what? Since "the church is holy . . . therefore all . . . are called to holiness . . . this is the will of God, your sanctification"

(*LG*, 39). It is important to notice that this text doesn't say that the church is called to be holy but rather that since it is already holy (for reasons spelled out in the above paragraphs) its members are called to holiness. In the very next number the council presses the issue: "Be perfect as my heavenly Father is perfect [means that Christians are to] hold on to and perfect in their lives that sanctification which they have received from God"; they are to live "as is fitting among the saints" (*LG*, 40). So, holiness is not only a fact, something "they have received from God," but also a call to house, to make a home for what God has initiated.

Is giving such an exalted stature to the church confirmed by personal experience? Hardly! What are we to do with our ever present, all too painful awareness of the sinfulness of the church? The usual way of handling this conundrum is to create an abstraction, an ahistorical and nonempirical church. Once we abstract its holiness from the church, we are left with something we can disdain, usually by calling it the institutional church. This split is a false one, however, since it is this institution that is the primary locus of God's holiness.

Another common way to explain away the church's sinfulness is to contend that the holiness of the church is a future thing and that during our sojourn on earth the only part of the church that can be considered holy is its head and not its body. But this isn't kosher either; the dichotomy is just more subtle than the previous one. *Lumen Gentium* addresses this protestantization of ecclesiology directly by describing the holiness of the pilgrim church as "real though imperfect" (*LG*, 48). Of course the fullness of the mark of holiness is a future event, as are the other marks, one, catholic, and apostolic. But to reduce the holiness of the church to its head and to the body's future is to denigrate what God has been doing in the church all these centuries. It's not the body-to-be that is holy; it is the body-that-is. To think otherwise is a refusal to accept the validity of the tradition's self-understanding about the holiness of the church. The council did not hesitate to admit that there is a dialectic about this, that the church is "at once holy and always in need of purification, [hence she] follows constantly the path of penance and renewal" (*LG*, 8).

In these several acknowledgments by the council more is going on than meets the eye. The German-Austrian Episcopal Conference, for which Karl Rahner was appointed a *peritus* (consultant), had introduced the idea to the council of naming the church the people of God. It did this in order to have the church treated much more historically and as existentially moving through time toward its goal, which is the glory of God. The council, in general, accepted this strongly proposed suggestion. It was the more credible for having done so since we moderns are much more attuned to historical realities than we are to ahistorical essences like a holy body unsoiled by time, history, and its own members.

The bride of Christ, a third image of the church used by the council, is probably even a better image for understanding the relationship between Christ and his members in this matter of holiness than the people of God or the body of Christ. It conveys the duality (not dualism) of two, the person of Christ and the bride, so they are obviously not one and the same. This bride of Christ is, furthermore, in a foreign land and in exile away from the Bridegroom. She seeks and is concerned about "what is above, where Christ is seated at the right hand of God," knowing all the while that her intending is not that obvious even to her in time and history because "the life of the Church is hidden with Christ in God until she appears in glory with her spouse" (Col. 3:1–4; *LG*, 6). There was no triumphalism in the council's ecclesiology, because the church "in her sacraments and institutions" is described as "belonging to this present age, and carries the mark of this world which will pass, [as] she herself takes her place among the creatures which groan and travail yet await the revelation of the sons of God" (Rom. 8:19–22; *LG*, 48). It sounds to me like the council introduced a fifth mark of the church here, one, holy, catholic, apostolic, but earthy, of earth.

This tension is similar to one of the challenges Jesus faced when he preached in his hometown of Nazareth: "Is he not the carpenter, the son of Mary, and the brother of James and Joses and Judas and Simon?" they asked incredulously (Mark 6:3). Familiarity can breed contempt or, at least, seeing according to old patterns can make us blind to the newness of the origins of the messenger. The everydayness of his humanity concealed his eternal divinity. How could humanity mediate divinity? We believe it did in the case of Christ. This is at the core of the Christian faith. Can the humanity of the church mediate the divinity of God? It seems it can if Christ's love of the church was like that of a husband who so loved his wife that he "handed himself over for her to sanctify her, cleansing her by the bath of water with the word, that he might present to himself the church in splendor, without spot or wrinkle or any such thing" (Eph. 5:25–27). Apparently his choice of her lifted her into a spousal status with him "so much did he love her." He was/is not ignorant of her need to be continually purified. Is he not in the process of bathing his bride by the power of the word even now? His intention is her holiness, and he is following through with this intention even now. Who of us would deny that our personal experience is ever twofold, that is, not only of how much more bathing each of us needs, but also of how successful Jesus continues to be in purifying us by the power of his word and the sacraments? I think, if we don't love this church that God is making holy, we will not love holiness.

To love the church we must love what Christ has chosen to make her and is making her and will be successful in making her. What is that? It is easier to see in the eschatological scenes Scripture provides. From the book of Revelation: "Come here. I will show you the bride, the wife of the Lamb. He took me in spirit to a great, high mountain and showed me the holy city Jerusalem coming down out of heaven from God" (Rev. 21:9–10). The vision is of this holy city "gleam[ing] with the splendor of God. Its radiance was like that of a precious stone, like jasper, clear as crystal" (21:11). But not to be missed is what is at the base of this splendor—twenty-four hairy ankles: "The wall of the city had twelve courses of stones as its foundation, on which were inscribed the twelve names of the twelve apostles of the Lamb" (21:14). To love the church is to love her in her dual reality, notwithstanding the slow purification, now centuries old, in process and still not completed.

Maybe the biggest obstacle to loving the holy church is our inability to see the beam in our own eye by our judgments of others or by our unwillingness to forgive one another's sins so that God can get on with the purification of each of us. It is only the blood of the Lamb that makes each of us whiter than snow. For the church is not a thing but a people in the process of being made a holy people in Christ through the Spirit. To love holiness, therefore, we must love the church's people. To love the church we must love what is a work in progress. This is not loving an abstraction or a hope but a holy, here-and-now reality, the slowness of whose purification mirrors the slowness of our own. It is far easier to find fault with the church than with ourselves. But conversely, it is also difficult to have any aspiration to personal holiness when we fail to believe in the holiness of the collectivity that is the church. This collectivity is a collection of people, like each of us, who are already and not yet holy. Like each of us, the church is holy and, at the same time, in a process of purification that is not yet complete.

The specific challenge in this material is to love the institutional church, the church that too many people—even believers—seem to love to hate. You may ask: How could someone love an institution about which so many horror stories are known and told daily? Take, for example, one of the worst-case scenarios, the sexual violation of pre-pubescent children by some priests. Doesn't this point to a rot at the core of "the institution"? The more empirical data one gathers, the more difficult it becomes to love the church.

We must challenge ourselves to get beyond this impasse. It seems to me that the more empirical one gets, the more encompassing one's empirical data must be before being sure of one's judgment. Let us take the most challenging case, that of pedophilic priests. Without ignoring the enormous harm done by these men to children, one must be open to all the empirical data. First of all, there was a societywide ignorance about this kind of pathology until the last decade or two. Sharing in that ignorance, bishops and perpetrators alike naively presumed that religious means, like confession, would take care of this supposedly "moral problem."

By this reductionism to the moral, both parties were deceived. Second, some of the priests I know who have been patients at the treatment centers established to treat this pathology have attested to the helpfulness of the therapy and to the depth of conversion that has been made possible to them through the psychological and psychoanalytic skills made accessible in such centers. Third, the fact that pedophilia is objectively a criminal act should not protect the priest perpetrator from the law. But there must not be still a further reductionism by seeing these acts simply in criminal terms. Reducing them either to criminal or immoral acts misses their pathological character. Is it unrealistic to hope for the day when the competence of the civil authorities for handling such matters, the skills of the therapeutic profession, and the means of conversion available through the church could all be combined under one tent, so to speak, for *all* of those afflicted by this deviant behavior?

I believe that many bishops covered up the problem in their concern not to scandalize the faithful about pedophilia, this most embarrassing of blemishes on the body of Christ. At the core of this cover-up was not an old boys' club mentality, it would seem, but a blindness to the fact that the holiness of the church was not meant to have us see ourselves as superior to others, nor immune from deviancy. Rather, holiness was not and is not meant to terminate in the church. It is for the world! God's holiness cannot be contained and is not to be parochialized by humans, episcopal or otherwise, who would confine it to members of the church, as if any of us could take credit for it. God's holiness in humans is for the glory of God, which is realized insofar as all human beings become fully alive to their dignity and eternal worth. Christ's own flesh has been crucified for the life of the world (John 6:51).

I have been stressing holiness as a gift up to this point. It is also a task entailing particular actions necessary for the gift to be credible to the world. To stay with this one situation of pedophilia, more complex tasks are necessary than prelates asking forgiveness to an undifferentiated mass of laity. While cheap grace takes no action, dear grace has to work persistently at the deep effects of the violation if a victim's healing is to be expected, similar to the effort invested in a twelve-step program. But interpersonally, for those who were victims as children and have reached their adult years unhealed, it might be useful where this seems feasible and possible, to have perpetrator and victim come together in a supervised context, so that the victim can communicate the hurt the perpetrator has caused and experience the remorse of a perpetrator who is willing to beg forgiveness. But the perpetrator also has a story that must be heard. Though these betrayals of trust are unconscionable, for a healing to take place, the victim needs to understand the compulsory character of pedophilia. As for victims who are still children, they need to be listened to, most of all. So situations must be created where they are convinced it is safe to surface their hurt and trauma to those to whom they can entrust it.

In general, the church has too readily settled for litigious processes rather than for spiritual ones in its attempts to begin the reconciliation and healing process. Litigation imposes from outside of the parties affected a settlement, an order, usually financial, that does not enable both parties to participate in what could eventually become a reconciliation. What the world needs to see is that "where sin increased, grace overflowed all the more" (Rom. 5:20).

If we are to be one in mind and heart with the Bridegroom, we must loathe the sins of the church, knowing all too well that each of us has been, and always will be, in desperate need of purification and conversion. God removes the stains and wrinkles, not the bride with them. Do we really believe God stops loving these priests? Injustice and violence should make us outraged, but no healing will occur if we stop there. We must be ready to forgive and to do so knowing we can never be holy if we deny the presence of stains within us as individuals and within the community as a whole. If we forget this, the real locus of holiness that is the church will not be loved, and instead a shredded, privatized concept of holiness will be the fruit of this error.

The moment the actual church is most herself is at the eucharistic meal. This is where we come, such as we are, in all of our individual and collective limitations, to be healed and where we seek to become a holier people once again. It is at Eucharist that the congregation eats food that is real food in all its empirical reality, yet it is more than that. It is where it drinks what is real drink in all its empirical reality, yet it is more than that. Here the challenge of holiness is held aloft for all to see. Here we are challenged to see more than what the visible reality presents to us. Here we are challenged to accept that the eucharistic meal unites all members—sinner and saint, as each of us is. In the Eucharist, Christ does not gloss over the tension between humanity and divinity but glories in it. By the mingling of the water and wine we are allowed to share in his divinity who has shared in our humanity, such as it is. We are not made holy by any abstraction but by what is as much food and drink as we are flesh and blood.

In this chapter I have introduced the initial idea of the challenge of holiness. A reader has a personal history both remote and immediate to these ideas. That history has much to do with how one has been catechized or brought up in the Christian faith. It also probes one's present spiritual condition, as well as one's fidelity or infidelity to grace. Finally, it probes one's heart for the desire for holiness. Or, perhaps, the lack of such a desire. If you feel up to the challenge, I invite you to explore these matters more deeply with me, as I journey through history.

2

Israel's Call to Holiness

IN THIS CHAPTER WE WILL examine Israel's understanding of and response to Yahweh's call to holiness. What did Israel understand by these words: "Be holy, for I, the LORD, your God, am holy" (Lev. 19:2)? Such a simple question, such a complex answer. Holiness for Israel was not a concept but a call, a call that has never been revoked (Rom. 11:29). It was a call delivered within a story. In this chapter I will attempt to tell the story in its simplicity so that we may hear again the summons it continues to deliver.

So as not to lose a sense of the call, I have chosen to treat only a portion of what is most representative and, therefore, not all the germane material.[1] Even with the material I have selected, I will be neither exegetical nor exhaustive but will stay within the story line. Since God's holiness is infinite and unfathomable, the communication of it to Israel was a story to be heard in order to be inhabited by both old and new Israel. One will hear little of, much less care for, the story if one is unwilling to enter it. First, it invites and inspires migration away from other stories that organize one's attention, inhabitation, and subsequent participation. This is a

35

story of God's holiness seeking to come to rest on a people. It not only informs but also forms. It folds receptive hearers into the people who have heard and responded to the call to holiness.

The story of God's holiness is told in human words, but it can't be heard without God's coming to our assistance. Without this assistance it will either be misheard or not heard at all. The variety of scenarios, images, notions, people, and authors involved in this story will make sense only if the hearer believes that ultimately they come from one Author who inspired many different people to convey the message. My choice of biblical books and the portion selected from each of them add something cumulative to the story line. Each portion of the selected books has a particular thread to weave into the rich fabric of the story of God's holiness in Israel. Each book, of course, represents different moments of Israel's history and, therefore, very different contexts and social locations. The construction of each book is quite complex with regard to authorship, as well as the place and time of composition. Consequently, one has to subscribe to the idea of divine inspiration by means of which the authors interpreted their particular circumstances in the way God wanted them to. Thus, in this chapter we will read human understandings of God's infinite holiness in its rich dimensionality, and they will be fit together into a single megastory or metanarrative.

The story is told chronologically, but it was not written that way. For example, in the next section the first three selections are taken from the Pentateuch, that is, the first five books of the Torah, which gives a sweeping panorama beginning with the creation of the world and ending with Moses and the Israelites on the plains of Moab facing the land of promise to which Moses has led them.[2] The actual composition of the Pentateuch did not begin until Israel's exile in Babylon. The Pentateuch's "schema seems to focus on the building of the Second Temple and the reestablishment of the cult after the return from exile"(Blenkinsopp, 51). This would mean that the Pentateuch functioned as a civic constitution for Judaism as it consolidated itself at the time of the Second Commonwealth (in the second century B.C.E.).

Original Justice

The founding story for Israel, Genesis 1–11, is basic to Israel's understanding of God. The book opens with an account of faith that is cosmic in scope, one that spans time and eternity in its depth. Israel's God is the Creator of all that is.[3] Israel, of course, was not alone as a people in developing stories of origin. As with other early peoples, for Israel to have an account of their origin was all the philosophy and theology they needed, since a story of origin conveyed their deity's purposes. In two ways their founding story differed from others: Israel's God came to be seen as the Creator of all that is, and all that was created is seen as "good," in fact, "very good" (Gen. 1:31). From the outset we are presented with a deep orientation to our subject: God's creation is good, and, therefore, how it is to be seen and used is to be determined by these a priori principles.

According to the inspired story, humans were unique among all the creatures whom God called into being and called good. They understood this about themselves and knew that they alone of all created things were described as blessed by God (Gen. 5:2). What this blessing was, for Adam and Eve, is not stated in the text. Centuries later, theologians described this blessing as an original justice whereby humans were created in a condition of being in right relationship with God. They were commissioned to "cultivate and care for" the Garden of Eden where God strolled (Gen. 2:15; 3:8).

Curiously, although all that God made was said to be good, only one thing is described as holy in the creation account. It was a day, the seventh day. God blessed it and made it holy (Gen. 2:3). God's intention was to have Israel learn to imitate God by resting on the seventh day, thereby seeing and experiencing the divine source of all that had been made available to them. By entering into rest with God on the day made holy, human beings would have a weekly experience of the origin and order of things and thereby live in a greater communion with the Holy One.

But things got out of hand from the start, as far as human response to the plan was concerned. "Adam and Eve" contravened the order of things and were expelled from the garden to the east of Eden, where hardship rather than the intended bounty was their lot. Good-bye, original justice! Their sons, Cain and Abel, begin to make the disorder their parents had bequeathed to them even more obvious. The preciousness of human life to God is stated forcefully when Cain is excoriated for his murder of Abel. "Your brother's blood cries out to me from the soil . . . that opened its mouth to receive your brother's blood from your hand. . . . [Consequently] you shall become a restless wanderer on the earth" (Gen. 4:10–12).

By chapter 6 of Genesis, God regrets having made anything at all because humans had sunk to such depravity and determines to "destroy them and all life on earth" (Gen. 6:13). But fortunately the divine anger is momentary; Noah and his wife represent a new beginning of the drama of God's relationship with humans. God's recommitment is now in the form of a "covenant with [Noah] and [his] descendants after [him] and with every living creature that was with [him]" (Gen. 9:9–10). Yahweh is now pictured not only as a Creator but also as committed to creation. Making a covenant with Noah was God's commitment to all creation to stay the course begun with creation. Henceforth, all the subsequent nations of the earth are traceable back to Noah in the story.

This story of origin begins a new chapter with Abram. Abram, soon to be Abraham, came to be credited with the spiritual condition Adam and Eve had enjoyed in the beginning. He was deemed right with God because he believed. "Abram put his faith in the LORD, who credited it to him as an act of righteousness" (Gen. 15:6). God promised that through Abraham "all the communities of the earth/shall find blessing" (Gen. 12:3). The scope is still as cosmic as it was with Noah, but the blessing's transmission is contingent on humans being right with God by believing, as Abraham had. Original justice returns to earth.

The Exodus

By the time we get to the book of Exodus, the picture is clearer about how all the nations of the earth are to be blessed. Now there is to be a nation that, like Abraham, will be righteous, and from this spiritual condition of being right with God by believing, this nation will be called to be holy. Israel is that nation, but Israel will also have to be taught the moral normativity necessary for it to be the instrument God intends for the plan of God to succeed. Before Israel, human history tended in the direction of one long departure from the ways of God—an *exitus a Deo,* if you will—into greater and greater malice toward one another and distance from God and from the truth that was available. God intervened before the chaos could be total, and with Israel, there began the *reditus ad Deum,* the return to God. But the return to God, the way of life that will enable the return to God, is spelled out beginning with the second book of the Pentateuch, Exodus.

In Exodus the call to holiness begins to take a more definite shape. We are now beyond the stories of the patriarchs, of Abraham,

Isaac, and Jacob—not to mention Joseph—as they were told in the book of Genesis. In Exodus, Israel is now a people under the oppression of the Pharaoh in Egypt. The story of their passage through the Red Sea is familiar to all. Israel is warned never to forget "how I bore you up on eagle wings and brought you here [to Sinai] to myself. Therefore, if you hearken to my voice and keep my covenant, you shall be my special possession, dearer to me than all other people, though all the earth is mine. You shall be to me a kingdom of priests, a holy nation" (Exod. 19:4–6). Israel's way of life with God is made very specific to Moses on Sinai. The stipulations in Exodus are moral, religious, and liturgical.

The God whom Moses encounters on Sinai is extremely serious, even to the point of being adamant, about this matter of holiness. Thunder, lightning, trumpet blasts, and a smoking mountain were the pyrotechnics that accompanied God's word to Israel about the specifics of the way of life Israel was to live. Moses informs the people that "God has come to you only to test you and put his fear upon you, lest you should sin" (Exod. 20:20). Sin now emerges as the enemy of the holiness God intends for Israel (and for all peoples through Israel). Sin is having "other gods besides me" (Exod. 20:3). There is the quality of totality in this Sinai theophany. "Do not make anything to rank with me; neither gods of silver nor gods of gold shall you make for yourselves" (Exod. 20:23). When they make a golden calf, Yahweh is furious and ready to destroy the people. God pleads to Moses, "Let me alone . . . that my wrath may blaze up against them to consume them" (Exod. 32:10).

It becomes clear in Exodus that God's intention is to make Israel a holy nation. But it is interesting how the text describes any number of things as holy, beginning with the "holy ground" Moses is told he is standing on as he beholds the burning bush. Throughout Exodus, holiness is predicated of places and garments and vessels and assemblies and oil and crowns and the ark and the tablets and the commandments and the dwelling and altars. All of these are intimations of how God's holiness is preparing Israel to become "a kingdom of priests, a holy nation. This is what you [Moses] must tell the Israelites" (Exod. 19:6). There are two emphases in Exodus that will accomplish this purpose. One of these is moral: to know and keep the commandments. The other is liturgical. Israel is to celebrate in its assemblies the deeds of God done on its behalf by Yahweh. Israel is to develop a keen awareness of these deeds by its enactment of the stories of those deeds.

As in Genesis, so also in Exodus, one thing seems to have been holy par excellence: the seventh day, the Sabbath. But now it becomes a more defined discipline. Of all the disciplines God mandates, the weekly observance of Sabbath had a preeminent place in the people's process of learning how to respond to the call and inhabit the story of holiness God intended for Israel. The Sabbath was the day when God's favor was to be especially enjoyed, God's voice was to be most audible, and God's name was to be most fully praised. Abraham Joshua Heschel's classic work on the Sabbath is a profound meditation from the Jewish tradition on Sabbath keeping and its relationship to holiness. He saw Sabbath as a cathedral built in time, into every seventh day.[4] If one enters this seventh day observantly, one enters into the sphere of God's holiness in time. By observing the Sabbath, Israel will come to know that "the precious thing which Thou wilt give us if we obey Thy Torah . . . [is] the world to come." The future world that is still to come "will be all Sabbath and rest in the life eternal. . . . The world to come is characterized by the kind of holiness possessed by the Sabbath in this world" (Ibid., 73).

Heschel's meditation on the Sabbath indicates how much the Hebrew Bible has to teach us about holiness. "To the philosopher the idea of the good is the most exalted idea. But to the Bible the idea of the good is penultimate; it cannot exist without the holy.

The good is the base, the holy the summit." Heschel continues: "things created in six days He considered *good; the seventh day He made holy.*" Even the survival of the world of nature depends on the holiness of the seventh day. "Without holiness there would be neither greatness nor nature." Our spirits and souls must "soar to eternity and aspire to the holy." How? "The Sabbath is an ascent to the summit. It gives us the opportunity to sanctify time, to raise the good to the level of the holy, to behold the holy by abstaining from the profane" (Ibid., 75–76).

Deuteronomy

This is the fifth and last book of the Pentateuch. It is written as if its words were voiced on the plains of Moab after the Israelites had crossed the Red Sea and before they crossed the river Jordan. But, in reality, it was written long after they had settled in the land of promise. The storyline, however, which we continue to honor has Moses, as God's spokesman, instructing the Israelites on how they are to be when they inhabit the land Yahweh has prepared for them. Canaan will be a blessing for them if they obey the words Moses imparts to them. It will be a curse if they don't.

Moses' instructions, spoken authoritatively as if they were from the mouth of God, articulate a complete way of life for his hearers before they enter Canaan. It castigates the syncretism and unfaithfulness Israel will be guilty of if, after they settle down in Canaan, they become enmeshed in the local population's myths, religions, and sanctuaries. If this happens Israel's metanarrative or deep story will lose its pith and coherence. The loyalties of its people will diffuse. So serious will the dilution be that this literary construct exhorts cruel treatment, even death, for anyone who leads the people into apostasy. It predicts the razing of a city if these religious abominations take place in them (Deut. 13). Central to this version of holiness is loyalty, undivided loyalty, complete commitment—in a word, covenant faithfulness.

The framework used by Deuteronomy for treating holiness is covenant. I have always appreciated Walter Bruggemann's explanation of covenant as embrace, the embrace of the people God had chosen to be "his own."[5] It takes two to make an embrace. Deuteronomy spells out how and why Israel is to respond to the covenant initiated by Yahweh. Why they are to respond is simple enough: because they have been chosen. How they are to respond: "Observe these statutes and decrees . . . with all your heart and with all your soul. Today you are making this agreement with the LORD: he is to be your God and you are to walk in his ways and observe his statutes, commandments and decrees, and to hearken to his voice" (Deut. 26:16–17). It would be loathsome to God if they were only to go through the motions of an embrace with something less than their hearts and souls in it. Many of the pious got stuck in the letter of the law and its observance. We can easily misunderstand Deuteronomic holiness if we see it mainly as a matter of observing statutes and so on.

A virtual theocracy is being envisioned by the authors of Deuteronomy. God's law is to permeate every area of life. For example, judges and officials are upbraided for taking bribes and not doing justice (Deut. 16:18–20). The king and his army are to desist from international adventurism (Deut. 17:16–17). The king is to take as his primary task the study of the law. God's law and it alone will make a nation worthy of the covenant. Worship is to be centralized and the "high places" of Canaan's gods, which have seduced the people into syncretism, are to be destroyed.

Deuteronomy plunges holiness into love. The embrace was to be one of love. Holiness was not to be something snagged by the law and the letter of the law. So often Israel's responses fell short of love, attending to externals. But since God has chosen you out of love, you are to respond in kind (Deut. 7:8). Holiness in the Deuteronomist understanding is unintelligible if its genesis does not begin in the heart of God and end in the response in love of the human heart. This response of love is spelled out in a way that is unmistakable in the famous Shema. "Hear, O Israel! . . . you shall love the LORD, your God, with all your heart, and with all your soul, and with all your strength" (Deut. 6:4–5). Notice the word *all*. Israel's God is a jealous God.

It is important to appreciate the innovative character of this Deuteronomic way of understanding God and holiness. Putting love rather than dread at the center of their response to this deity was without parallel in the history of religions. Yahweh's love for this people was what generated the covenant, so this people's love for Yahweh was to complete the circle.

The certainty that they were loved would be reinforced as often as they remembered and celebrated the acts of love that had made them a people, beginning with the Exodus. And the land they had settled in, "a land with fine, large cities that you did not build, with houses full of goods of all sorts that you did not garner, with cisterns that you did not dig, with vineyards and olive groves that you did not plant" (Deut. 6:10–11)—insofar as they remembered who gave them this land, their love would be the response. Love (God's) began the story, and love (Israel's) would bring it full circle. Moses set before Israel a stark either–or: either "life and prosperity, [or] death and doom" (Deut. 30:15). "Choose life, then, that you and your descendants may live, by loving the LORD, your God, heeding his voice, and holding fast to him. For that will mean life for you, a long life for you to live on the land which the LORD swore he would give to your fathers Abraham, Isaac and Jacob" (Deut. 30:19–20).

Deuteronomy's sense of God is that of "a numinous presence," whose character is one of "divine compassion and election" (Gammie, 113). The power of this numinous presence was conveyed with awe-inspiring symbols—fire, smoke, cloud, voice, and darkness. But these symbols were used to evoke a response that was to be a love admixed with a reverence that approached the kind of fear appropriate to the stakes involved, "life or death." "For what great nation . . . has gods so close to it as the LORD, our God, is to us whenever we call upon him?" This awe-inspiring God was most evident to the people in the "whole law which I am setting before you today" (Deut. 4:7–8). The primary mode of presence of the awesome God was to be God's "voice," which was to be heard in "all his commandments which I now enjoin on you" (Deut. 30:8). But they were to see all these commandments as addressed to their hearts:

> For this command which I enjoin on you today is not too mysterious and remote for you. It is not up in the sky, that you should say "Who will go up in the sky to get it for us and tell us of it, that we may carry it out?" Nor is it across the sea, that you should say, "Who will cross the sea to get it for us and tell us of it, that we may carry it out?" No, it is something very near to you, already in your mouths and in your hearts; you have only to carry it out. (Deut. 30:11–14)

Your flourishing will depend on your acceptance of the embrace that I your God have initiated, Deuteronomy is saying.

I should note one very significant peculiarity about this Deuteronomic understanding of holiness. The term holy (*qaμdôπ*) is rarely used in the book of Deuteronomy, and it is never used of God *solo,* nor is it used of the divine name, nor of the spirit. Apparently, this is because holiness by now is a relational, divine/human kind of reality in the mind of the authors. Israel's holiness was contingent on its response to carrying out its side of the covenant. Israel was invited to inhabit the story, so to speak, and thereby ratify God's choice of a people. For them to be a holy people they had to allow themselves to be enfolded into the embrace God had initiated and invited. Then they would be "a people [holy] to the LORD" (Deut. 7:6; 14:2, 21). We now conclude with the Pentateuch.

Separation from the Profane

We come now to the prophets. Ezekiel, the author of the book that bears his name, was exiled into Babylon along with the rest of vanquished Israel in 597 B.C.E. He became a prophet with such authority he has been called the father of Judaism. His understanding of holiness is representative of the priestly school's angle of vision on the subject. That school understood holiness in terms of separation. Those who were chosen by God were to keep separate from all the ways that were hostile to God, or disobedient or unfaithful to God's call to holiness. The separation from the profane was to be total.

Although Deuteronomy had already begun to dwell on the theme of God's name, the most distinguishing thing about Ezekiel's understanding of God is about the Name. It is God's Name that separates Israel from the profane. It has been spoken on earth, to Israel alone, and has remained immanent in Israel. Israel is the people of God because they have been chosen to hear and bear God's Name. Israel is called to forsake its former way of life because it has come into a space made sacred by the Name of the Lord. This Name has created a field of force, the sacredness of which separates Israel from the nations. This Name brings together the created and the uncreated, the immanent and the transcendent, the divine and the human, into a realm made one by God's holiness. When Israel acts contrary to God's will, God will act with zeal "for my name's sake." All of God's punitive actions are taken to preserve the holiness of the Name by purifying the people who bear responsibility for it, according to Ezekiel. So, sixty-three times in the book of Ezekiel God reacts to Israel's infidelities with a promise of punishment, "so that you may know that I am the Lord."

The clearest example of the tug-of-war between Israel's acts and God's response to them is in Ezekiel 20:1–26. Here God is depicted as venting about the three different times that "I revealed myself to them and swore: I am the LORD, your God" (Ezek. 20:5) and was scorned. The first time was in Egypt, when they refused to "throw away . . . the detestable things that have held your eyes" (Ezek. 20:7), but by sparing them, "I acted for my name's sake, that it should not be profaned in the sight of the nations" (Ezek. 20:9). The second time was in the desert after "I gave them my statutes and made known to them my ordinances . . . [and] my sabbaths to be a sign between me and them, to show that it was I, the LORD, who made them holy" (Ezek. 20:11–12). But, once again, after "they despised my ordinances . . . [and desecrated] my sabbaths," (Ezek. 20:13) God relented a second time and brought them into the land flowing with milk and honey. The third time the same kind of invitation was extended, this time to the next generation, "to their children," (Ezek. 20:18) but with the same results. "But I stayed my hand, acting for my name's sake, lest it be profaned in the sight of the nations" (Ezek. 20:22). Nevertheless, because they had "eyes only for the idols of their fathers," they were dispersed into exile in Babylon. They adopted evil statutes from the cultures around them, with the result that they were "defiled by their gifts, by their immolation of every first-born" (Ezek. 20:24, 26).

Name, therefore, is the key to understanding Ezekiel's theology of holiness. The ancient world understood names differently than moderns do. As with many ancient peoples, the name bore the whole reality of the person named. There was great reluctance, therefore, to state one's name to another if there was no certainty about whether the recipient would reverence it or defame it. One can see this same reserve in the Old Testament, wherein God reveals his Name slowly and circumspectly. So God's name is revealed to Abraham (Gen. 17:1) and then to Moses (Exod. 6:2), since they are the first main carriers of the story of holiness to the people of the Name. As God's plan unfolded, God's ineffable Name was to come to rest in a place "which the LORD, your God, chooses as the dwelling place for his name" (Deut. 12:11). Israel was that place. This is why there had to be a separation from those who had not received the Name.

Ezekiel came to see that God was now, by choice, in a very vulnerable spot, since Israel had been given the Name. God had created a relationship of unprecedented intimacy by this decision. It is this vulnerability that explains why God jealously guards the Name, which, in a sense, posited the inner being of the transcendent God with a people. But they had become coarse, even though they had been accorded such an unprecedented dignity. In the first twenty-four chapters of Ezekiel, an Israel in exile is reproached for its sinful disregard of its specialness to God. But an even greater catastrophe is experienced once the exiles learn of the destruction of the temple in Jerusalem. Its destruction shook exiled Israel's faith to its very roots because it seems that they had come to believe that the temple itself, rather than the name housed in a people, was the assurance of God's unfailing presence to them. It belonged to Ezekiel to disabuse them of their misunderstanding. Ezekiel was able to teach them that the glory and Name of God are inextricably linked rather than the Name and the temple. This glory/Name linkage proves to be an important development, since it dismantles Israel's edifice complex. Even more important, it prepares them for a personal Messiah who will be invested with divine glory and will restore the radiance lost by all the deviance Israel had brought to the dwelling place of the Name. The glory/Name linkage gives God more mobility, so to speak, than the temple/Name linkage did for divinity's future dealings with humanity.

Israel's return from the Babylonian exile happens because God again has a change of heart. "I have relented because of my holy name which the house of Israel profaned among the nations where they came. . . . Not for your sakes do I act, house of Israel, but for the sake of my holy name" (Ezek. 36:21–22). It is as if God's own reality is defiled by idolatry and unfaithfulness. Two realities cannot coexist: the holiness of God and an unholy nation. When they do, either God has to separate from what is an abomination to God, or Israel has to be purified first through the expiation for its sins (by exile in this case) and then by being separated once again from the profane nations in returning to its own land. It is through the return from exile that "I will prove the holiness of my great name. . . . Thus the nations shall know that I am the LORD, says the Lord GOD, when in their sight I prove my holiness through you" (Ezek. 36:23).

Even at this great distance, this divine decision should be marveled at. Having taken the chance of revealing and committing what was most intimately God's, the Name, to a people whose response to the revelation was somewhere between indifferent and utterly coarse, why didn't God decide to turn Israel loose to fend for itself, a course that would have led to its certain destruction? Wouldn't God have been wiser by annulling the committal of the divine Name and thereby have ceased to be vulnerable? This would have returned the holy Name back to heaven, thereby ensuring its inviolability. Surely this would have made sense, since Israel had proven to be morally bankrupt. But God, almost incomprehensibly, chose to stay the course and continued to be vulnerable. We are used to celebrating God's power. This decision to stay with Israel should be a cause for real celebration. God didn't take his marbles and go home, as a "strong" God would have, but chose to be weak so as to continue with a partner who had so far proven to be most unworthy. This seems to be at the heart of what Ezekiel was given to see and say. It's what made him a prophet. It wouldn't be the last time God would choose the route of weakness so that humans could become strong.

The Name is God's favor come to rest on a people, in space and time. The people of God, on the strength of this now reissued Name, can now undertake their return from exile to enjoy again God's favor. But Ezekiel's God has another surprise to convey to a people now chastened by exile. An extraordinary promise is soon made that trumps even what would seem to have been the last card God could have played, having made a people a carrier of the divine Name. This new promise is: "I will give you a new heart and place a new spirit within you, taking from your bodies your stony hearts and giving you natural hearts. I will put my spirit within you and make you live by my statutes, careful to observe my decrees. You shall live in the land I gave your fathers; you shall be my people, and I will be your God" (Ezek. 36:26–28). To put it anthropomorphically, God was in a bind, having given so much of "himself" to Israel. It would not have been unjust to set Israel adrift and go back to being God at a distance. But, mercifully for Israel and for all humanity, God chose to invest even more of "himself" by putting "my spirit within you." This is even more intimate than revealing his Name. Nonetheless, although Israel is the beneficiary of all this forbearance and unimaginable largesse, still Israel is reminded that "not for your sakes do I act, says the Lord GOD—let this be known to you!" (Ezek. 36:32). What does this "Name theology" have to do with holiness? If a people lives in the field of force that comes with this Name, and implores the Name, reverences the Name, uses the Name in both prayer and discourse about faith with neighbor, never takes the Name in vain, that people will do justice to the holiness of the Name. But further moral demands are made on those who enter this sphere of divine favor. The moral stipulations in Ezekiel are not original with him. They are part and parcel of the moral code issued at Sinai by Yahweh and delivered to Israel through Moses. In spelling out the particular way to walk within the Name, both morality and doxology fold into one.

For those who are curious about the actual names Israel used of God, a brief excursus here might be helpful before we proceed further. The matter of God's names is quite complex. Four different sources have been located by biblical scholarship to explain the construction of the Hebrew Scriptures. These are usually considered the J, E, P, and D sources (Yahwist, Elohist, Priestly, and Deuteronomic). Would that it were as simple as saying each of the four sources had a different name for God, but it isn't. Suffice it to say that the usual name for God in Israel was Yahweh. Whether this name was common before Moses or was revealed to Moses (Exod. 3:14) depends on different interpretations by scholars. It seems sure that in the era of the patriarchs God was named *Shaddai* or *El Shaddai*. It is also clear that late in the Old Testament *Adonai* was preferred for God's name, leaving YHWH unpronounced out of reverence. *Adonai* was considered the name of God arrived at by putting together the vowels left out of the consonants *yhwh*. *Elohim* is the most complicated of the names of God. It, or more often *El*, was used outside of Israel as a term for god(s) by those whose religions were polytheistic. It can be understood as singular or plural, gods or god, though when Israel used it, obviously, they signified that there was no *Elohim* like Yahweh. Finally, *Lord* (*Kyrios*) is the Septuagint (LXX Greek) rendering of the Hebrew Yahweh.

Add Justice and Universality

We continue here to explore the depths of Israel's understanding of holiness. Understanding it cannot be confined to one moment in God's revelation to Israel. Let's look at a second prophetic book, Isaiah. The reader might recall that in the book of Isaiah we have three different Isaiahs from three contiguous moments in that time of Israel's history, but there is one theology of holiness in the whole of Isaiah. All three Isaiahs are derived from the experience of first Isaiah, an individual, Isaiah of Jerusalem. In his vision he experienced himself as living in direct sight of the holiness of God. His vocation then was to call Israel to see that the Israelites too are living exposed to this same holiness.

In the year of the death of King Uzziah (742 B.C.E.) Isaiah of Jerusalem had a vision of "the Lord seated on a high and lofty throne, with the train of his garment filling the temple" (Isa. 6:1). The seraphim in this vision cry out to one another, "Holy, holy, holy is the LORD of hosts!" (Isa. 6:3). And from this direct vision of God it is clear that "all the earth is filled with his glory" (Isa. 6:3). While all the earth may be filled with God's glory, Israel is the most specially gifted portion of all God's creation. "The vineyard of the LORD of hosts is the house of Israel,/and the men of Judah are his cherished plant" (Isa. 5:7). The holiness initiated by the Holy One of Israel toward Israel is short-circuited when Israel is unjust. Injustices abort God's desire to choose Israel as "his own." "He looked for judgment, but see, bloodshed!/for justice, but hark, the outcry!" (Isa. 5:7). This link with justice is the main point of the understanding of holiness that we find in Isaiah. Israel's relationship with God must be one of being just and doing justice to one another. Otherwise "the train of his garment" is removed from the temple and from the people (Isa. 1:4; 5:18–19; 30:8–14). Having "grieved the Holy One of Israel" by their injustice, they will be forsaken.

Combined with the direct linkage of holiness with justice in Isaiah is an anticultic theme. The role that cult has taken is the other part of Isaiah's message to Israel. Israel has deceived itself precisely through its seeming devotion to God. "Trample my courts no more!/ Bring no more worthless offerings;/your incense is loathsome to me./New moon and sabbath, calling of assemblies,/octaves [liturgical weeks] with wickedness: these I cannot bear. . . ./Make justice your aim: redress the wronged,/hear the orphan's plea, defend the widow" (Isa. 1:13, 17). We are far beyond Ezekiel's priestly understanding of holiness here. The people are to be led to justice by their leaders, the king and the courts, who are to exercise right judgment (Isa. 11:3–5). They are to see to it that the poor and hungry are cared for (Isa. 11:4; 32:5–7). They are to oversee a cessation of all types of oppression (Isa. 1:16–17). Israel becomes clean in God's eyes not by ritual cleansing but by doing justice in this prophetic understanding of holiness. "When you spread out your hands [in prayer],/I close my eyes to you;/Though you pray the more,/I will not listen./Your hands are full of blood! . . ./Put away your misdeeds from before my eyes;/cease doing evil; learn to do good" (Isa. 1:15–17).

Thus, there is more than the relationship between God and Israel in this matter of holiness. It is a troika. There is to be a relationship of justice between Israelites themselves if they want to be in relationship with God. But there is also to be a relationship with other peoples, who are left otherwise nondescript in the texts except that they are the poor, like the widow, the orphan, the foreigner. The very character of God is at stake in this understanding of holiness. Hence, the haughty and arrogant shall be humbled and the mighty brought low, "but the LORD of hosts shall be exalted by his judgment,/and God the Holy shall be shown holy by his justice" (Isa. 5:16).

What Isaiah sees and teaches is that justice is intrinsic to holiness in God's eyes. When justice is wanting, God will purify

Israel until justice is done by her. This purification is best understood by God's responses to Isaiah's bewailing of personal unwor-
thiness upon his beholding the vision of God's holiness. "Woe is
me, I am doomed! For I am a man of unclean lips, living among a
people of unclean lips" (Isa. 6:5). One of the seraphim takes a
burning ember and touches Isaiah's mouth with it: "See . . . now
that this has touched your lips, your wickedness is removed, your
sin purged" (Isa. 6:7). This is a paradigmatic action because, as the
whole of Isaiah shows, the unholiness of Israel is not met by God's
flight but with purifying actions of cleansing. There is a pruning
with a view to a better yield from the vineyard or a threshing that
separates the kernel from the chaff.

As we found with Ezekiel, so we find with Isaiah, at the core
of the explication of the holiness theme, a messianic/christological
prophecy emerges. This prophecy foresees that after the exile only
a stump shall be left of the Davidic dynasty. But from this stump
a remnant or a shoot shall sprout, and a bud shall blossom forth
and "the spirit of the LORD shall rest upon him:/a spirit of wisdom
and of understanding,/A spirit of counsel and of strength,/a spirit of
knowledge and of fear of the LORD,/and his delight shall be the
fear of the LORD" (Isa. 11:2–3).

The result of the outpouring of these gifts of the Spirit on this
longed-for Messiah is that his holiness will show itself as justice.
Therefore, "Not by appearance shall he judge,/nor by hearsay shall he
decide,/But he shall judge the poor with justice,/and decide aright for
the land's afflicted. . . ./Justice shall be the band around his waist" (Isa.
11: 3–5). The ensuing peace and well-being are seen as very local but
with a vista that stretches to the ends of the earth. "There shall be no
harm or ruin on all my holy mountain;/for the earth shall be filled
with knowledge of the LORD,/as water covers the sea" (Isa. 11:9).

Isaiah heard the ache of God's heart for those within Israel
who were treated unjustly, just as God had heard the cry of

lamentation coming from Israel while she was still in Egypt and under the oppression of the Pharaoh. In both cases God promises to make manifest the deep bond God has with any who suffer. "The LORD of hosts shall be exalted by his judgment,/and God the Holy shall be shown holy by his justice" (Isa. 5:16). Not only were Israel's injustices perpetrated by individuals, they were also structural. Consequently, woe will be visited on those who, for example, "acquit the guilty for bribes,/and deprive the just man of his rights" (Isa. 5:23). As a result, the wrath of God will be unleashed on God's unfaithful-because-unjust people in the form of Assyria's successful invasion of Israel. The adjective that keeps occurring to me to describe Isaiah's vision of holiness is *large*. He saw holiness in large terms. First of all, those called to holiness are whole peoples *(a)* Israel; *(b)* the northern kingdom (Isa. 28); *(c)* King Ahaz, as representative of Judah (Isa. 7–8); *(d)* the southern kingdom after the fall of Samaria (Isa. 5); and *(e)* the remnant in Jerusalem after the devastation of 701 B.C.E. (Isa. 1). This remnant, the sliver left of a nation, will end up being the key instrumentality in the divine pursuit of making holiness a reality in the whole human order.

But *large* also in a second sense. The nations beyond Israel are first of all mere instruments for executing the justice-holiness plan of the Holy One of Israel. These instrumentalized nations in Isaiah were Assyria (Isa. 10:1–19), Philistia (Isa. 14:28–32), and Egypt (Isa. 19). When the strong nations of the earth are marshaled to implement Yahweh's will to have a people yield to holiness, one gets an idea of how high on God's agenda holiness is. But this use of national instruments vis-à-vis Israel can overlook an even more remarkable development. In Isaiah of Jerusalem, and then continued even more clearly in the other two Isaiahs, we see just how universal God's holiness plan is. Just as the glory of the Lord filled the whole earth (Isa. 6:3) in Isaiah's vision of God's holiness, so also will this holiness eventually suffuse even Israel's harshest enemies. Just as these nations had been God's instruments in the purification of Israel (Isa. 5:26–29; 7:18–19; 10:5–6), so these same nations will worship the Holy One of Israel.

The breadth of God's plan is breathtaking in Isaiah:

> The LORD shall make himself known to Egypt, and the Egyptians shall know the LORD in that day; they shall offer sacrifices and oblations. . . . On that day there shall be a highway from Egypt to Assyria; the Assyrians shall enter Egypt, and the Egyptians enter Assyria. . . . On that day Israel shall be a third party with Egypt and Assyria, a blessing in the midst of the land, when the LORD of hosts blesses it: "Blessed be my people Egypt, and the work of my hands Assyria, and my inheritance, Israel." (Isa. 19:21, 23–25)

What an irony! God's plan initially involves a separation from the unholy but with the intention of leaving no one outside of the ambit of this holy field of force. One can now see that there is a dialectic between the separation-from-the-profane note being played in the priestly account of holiness and the universal inclusion-of-the-separated note in the prophetic account of Isaiah. The first keeps holiness from becoming sloppy and presumptuous while the second keeps holiness from becoming exclusionary and sectarian. The first without the second would leave holiness prone to a vertical, pious religiosity. And the second without the first would leave holiness prone to activism and under the control of human agency. Doxology sanitizes social justice, and social justice tethers piety to the social condition in which people live.

To complete this picture of holiness in the book of Isaiah a brief comment needs to be made on the other two Isaiahs. With Deutero-Isaiah (the author is called Isaiah of Babylon, chs. 40–55) we can begin to see the universality of the holiness agenda become even more pronounced. Since Israel's Yahweh is now seen to be more clearly Creator of the universe than had been understood before the exile, the scope of the work God intends is that "all mankind shall see [the glory of the LORD] together" (Isa. 40:5). Paradigmatic of this universality will be the movement of the exiles out of Babylon back to their homeland and Jerusalem. This Creator God (43:15), who liberates the oppressed and is Israel's Redeemer, is now likened to "a shepherd [who] feeds his flock;/in his arms he gathers the lambs,/Carrying them in his bosom,/and leading the ewes with care" (Isa. 40:11). Back in their homeland the remnant is assured: "I will make of you a threshing sledge . . ./ To thresh the mountains and crush them,/to make the hills like chaff./When you winnow them, the wind shall carry them off/and the storm shall scatter them./But you shall rejoice in the LORD,/ and glory in the Holy One of Israel" (Isa. 41:15–16).

With Trito-Isaiah (he is called Isaiah of the Restoration, chs. 56–66) there is both continuity with the other two Isaiahs and discontinuity. Justice is still key, but while each Israelite must "do what is just; . . ./my justice [is] about to be revealed" (Isa. 56:1). What is added to the revelation of divine justice of First and Second Isaiah is insight into who will be included in the remnant community. "Let not the foreigner say,/when he would join himself to the LORD,/'The LORD will surely exclude me from his people';/Nor let the eunuch [originally excluded because of physical deformity] say [the same]. . . ./[To those who] choose what pleases me/and hold fast to my covenant,/I will give, in my house/and within my walls, a monument and a name/Better than sons and daughters . . ./I will give them" (Isa. 56:3–5). And the passage continues, "The foreigners who join themselves to the LORD,/ministering to him,/Loving the name of the LORD,/and becoming his servants . . ./Them I will bring to my holy mountain/and make joyful in my house of prayer. . . ./For my house shall be called/a house of prayer for all peoples" (Isa. 56:6–7).

These two emphases, one on universality and the other on inclusion of the marginal, heighten the need for holiness to be manifested by justice, as was already seen in first Isaiah. Therefore, for example, "This, rather, is the fasting that I wish:/releasing those bound unjustly,/untying the thongs of the yoke;/Setting free the oppressed . . ./and the homeless;/Clothing the naked when you see them,/and not turning your back on your own" (Isa. 58:6–7).

The Place of Suffering

With Job we come to the sixth and last piece about holiness that we will examine in this chapter. What is the connection between holiness and suffering? The book of Job is the obvious place to look for the answer. In the three cycles of speeches so many conflicting things are said by Job and his friends about why he is suffering that the holiness theme can easily be lost.

The book of Job has rightly been classified with the wisdom literature of the Hebrew Scriptures. It is representative of wisdom literature because it is instructive, universal, and didactic. It is instructive about how to understand human suffering by seeing how Job deals with it. It is universal because it culls from the wisdom of the sages of the ambient cultures to contribute to Israel's trove of wisdom. And it is also didactic without presuming that the hearer/reader has inhabited Israel's saving story. We know neither the identity nor the date of the composition of the book of Job—usually estimated to be sometime between the seventh and the fifth centuries B.C.E.

The Lord's comment to Satan about Job declares his goodness. "Have you noticed my servant Job, and that there is no one on earth like him, blameless and upright, fearing God and avoiding

evil?" (Job 1:8). Job's many ordeals follow. He surmises that they
are God's intentional acts toward him, but he is sure they cannot
be explained by his sins since "my hands are free from violence,/
and my prayer is sincere" (Job 16:17). But his friends are not convinced, and they say as much in the cycles of speeches, because in
their view God would not have allowed Job to suffer so unless he
were guilty of something. Their conviction about the direct connection between sin and suffering confounds Job, but Job persists
in his declaration of innocence: "My justice I maintain and I will
not relinquish it;/my heart does not reproach me for any of my
days" (Job 27:6).

By the third cycle of speeches, one of Job's friends, Eliphaz,
introduces the subject of wisdom into the reflection on suffering.
He moves beyond the subject of simply being right before God to
how one grows in wisdom. Job's wealth must be disesteemed,
Eliphaz tells him. "[If you] treat raw gold like dust,/and the fine gold
of Ophir as pebbles from the brook,/Then the Almighty himself
shall be your gold/and your sparkling silver" (Job 22:24–25). Job
concurs and sees the point in being tested as he was for having been
tried, "I should come forth as gold" (Job 23:10). Detachment from
and indifference about his resources enter the picture. Wisdom,
detachment, suffering, and holiness begin to mesh at this point in
the book. Having been stripped of his many possessions and of
what he had treasured, Job came to be able to count gold as dust.

Job's sufferings surface the question of God's wisdom. But
this only compounds the problem facing Job because it is the
seemingly remote character of this divine wisdom that becomes so
bewildering. If God is omniscient, how can suffering be explained,
especially undeserved suffering, the suffering of the innocent?
Apart from himself and his ordeals, Job wonders how to explain
the suffering of the poor, who have to forage for food or lie open
to the elements all night, now drenched, now freezing (Job 24).

How can God be called wise and fully aware of these very things without seeming to be insensitive or ineffectual or even cruel? How can a wise God let the murderer and the adulterer who commit their acts under cover of darkness go unpunished? Job's personal suffering, therefore, generates the larger problematic: How can this Holy God be wise and let such terrible things happen without doing something about them?

Not finding any clarity for his questions, Job undertakes a sensitive, multifaceted examination of conscience and comes out affirming his integrity. "For the dread of God will be upon me,/ and his majesty will overpower me" [if I am deceiving myself] (Job 31:23).[6] Again his detachment from his wealth is mentioned in this moral inventory. "Had I put my trust in gold/or called fine gold my security;/Or had I rejoiced that my wealth was great,/or that my hand had acquired abundance . . ./I should have denied God above" (Job 31:24–25, 28). Instead, he can affirm that God has become his wealth. His afflictions proved to be the beginning of wisdom for him. Growth in holiness is growth in wisdom here.

Nonetheless, he still has a ways to go. From chapter 32 to chapter 37 Elihu, another friend, begins to transcendentalize God's wisdom. He upbraids Job for talking too much to God, observing that in doing so "he is adding rebellion to his sin/by brushing off our arguments/and addressing many words to God" (Job 34:37). Elihu is sure that "Job to no purpose opens his mouth, and without knowledge multiplies words" (Job 35:16). By contrast, God "does great things beyond our knowing;/wonders past our searching out" (Job 37:5). Elihu has introduced the theme of humility into the text, since he is aware of how far God's thoughts and ways are from ours. "The Almighty! we cannot discover him,/pre-eminent in power and judgment;/his great justice owes no one an accounting./Therefore men revere him,/though none can see him, however wise their hearts" (Job 37:23–24).

Next, God begins to address Job and his friends after they have had their say and are still confused. The speech of God underscores the vast difference between God's omniscience and Job's ridiculously superficial knowledge of even natural things, much less the things of God. In chapters 38–39 God takes Job's complaints and turns them around into divine complaints about the deep limitations of Job's knowledge. Almost mockingly God asks: "Who is this that obscures divine plans/with words of ignorance? . . ./I will question you, and you tell me the answers" (Job 38:2–3). Job is informed that he does not see what God is doing in nature, so therefore how can he in anything else? For example, God asks Job whether he knows "the dwelling place of light,/and where is the abode of darkness" (Job 38:19), whether he has "entered into the sources of the sea,/or walked about in the depths of the abyss . . ./[or] entered the storehouse of the snow,/and seen the treasury of the hail" (Job 38:16, 22). "Which way to the parting of the winds?" (Job 38:24). "Has the rain a father;/or who has begotten the drops of dew?/Out of whose womb comes the ice,/ and who gives the hoarfrost its birth in the skies?" (Job 38:28–29). "Who provides nourishment for the ravens/when their young ones cry out to God?" (Job 38:41). God inquires of Job, "Is it by your discernment that the hawk soars,/that he spreads his wings toward the south?/Does the eagle fly up at your command/to build his nest aloft?" (Job 39:26–27).

Job's response to these divine taunts is a radical acknowledgment of his newly discovered ignorance and a confession about the woeful limitations of his knowledge:

> I know that you can do all things, and that no purpose of yours can be hindered. I have dealt with great things that I do not understand; things too wonderful for me, which I cannot know. I had heard of you by word of mouth, but now my eye has seen

you. Therefore I disown what I have said, and repent in dust
and ashes. (Job 42:2–6)

Job submits to the omniscience of God and repents for
listening to his own presumptions and the ignorance of his
friends, and for having leveled impious charges against the Holy
God. In all of this Job is growing through wisdom, detachment,
and humility to true holiness.

A chastened Job learns a reverent, awed appreciation verging
on fear of the complete otherness of God. With his mind, Job and
his friends had been presumptuous about bridging the unbridge-
able. It is not that God wanted Job to cease to wonder or question,
but the only way this "reason[ing] with God" (Job 13:3) could be
done with wisdom was if the great distance between God's
thoughts and their thoughts, God's ways and their ways, was
acknowledged. God needed to be left free to be God for Job, his
friends, and all creatures. This acknowledgment could not be
piecemeal but had to be woven into the very warp and woof of
their character.

In Job, fear of God was a quality that delighted God as he
commented to Satan that "there is no one on earth like him,
blameless and upright, fearing God and avoiding evil" (Job 1:8).
In fact, one could understand the whole book as an argument
between Job and God that God wins so that Job might grow in the
fear of the Lord, which had so delighted God in his precalamity
days. So what I find in this whole text is the connection between
suffering and holiness, which grows because of detachment,
humility, and fear of the Lord.

But even more central is the message that wisdom is
intrinsic to holiness in the book of Job. "But whence can wisdom be obtained,/and where is the place of understanding?"
Only "God knows the way to it;/it is he who is familiar with its

place" (Job 28:12, 23). Belittled by God's question to him: "Who is this that obscures divine plans with/words of ignorance?" (Job 38:2), Job finally confesses: "Behold, I am of little account; what can I answer you?/I put my hand over my mouth./Though I have spoken once, I will not do so again;/though twice, I will do so no more" (Job 40:4–5). The divine onslaught of questions (chs. 38–39) and comparisons (chs. 40–41) brings Job to admit, "I have dealt with great things that I do not understand;/things too wonderful for me, which I cannot know" (Job 42:3). Finally, "Therefore I disown what I have said,/and repent in dust and ashes" (Job 42:6). A good man has become wise, humble, detached, repentant. We are now ready for the sovereignty of holiness that is the kingdom of God.

3

Re-enchanting Jesus' Holiness

I F CHRISTIANS HAVE ANY ICON of human holiness, it would have to be Jesus. But we do a real disservice to ourselves, and to that embodiment of holiness, if he is raised up to inaccessible heights without his ever having been seen and experienced as one of us. An enchanted understanding of him needs to be deconstructed in order to bring him into the humanity he has in common with us. If our understanding of Jesus cannot be deconstructed, holiness will remain remote as an aspiration. By putting him on a pedestal, we might honor him and praise him, and even call him Lord, but we can't follow him if our images of him have placed him utterly beyond the pale of our humanity and out of sight of our human condition.

In this chapter I want to deconstruct or disenchant him so as to bring him down to the size of our humanity. I will do this because his holiness was really human. I want to establish two points: that he was a man of faith and that he learned the way we do, with a consciousness that is the same as ours. The fact that the

Spirit rested upon him doesn't differ in kind from what Christians have going for them in their learning process. Then I want to spell out how the Spirit enabled him and the early church to subsume all the disparate strands of holiness we saw in the previous chapter into one and into him. And, finally, I want to connect his authority to his holiness.

Methodologically, I will keep our inquiry as close to the experience of our human condition as possible in order to do justice to his humanity. If we fail to do justice to his humanity and do not find explanations of him that resonate with our human experience, then he becomes more and more unlike us. That would make his having become one of us futile. So, by this method of "Christology from below," a number of legitimate questions are raised that a "Christology from above" wouldn't think to ask. For example, did Jesus grow in holiness, or had he already attained it from the beginning? If we say that he grew in holiness, does that mean he was in some sense not yet holy or that he grew from unholiness into holiness? Was he somewhere between already holy but not yet so? If a not-yet-holy-Jesus is an intolerable perception to entertain, I believe we have transcendentalized him out of his humanity. In saying this I want to assure the reader that the classical dogmatic formula of the Council of Chalcedon (451) that defined Jesus as having two natures, divine and human, is part of our Christian faith. But since the subsequent tradition keyed on the divine nature to the neglect of his human nature—and did so for praiseworthy reasons, not the least of which was praise of him—we have some catching up to do. So, here, without denying his divinity, I want to focus on his humanity because that aspect of his mystery has been left underdeveloped until recent times.

The Faith of Jesus

One of the questions that has surfaced in recent christological scholarship is whether Jesus had faith. Christians have expended so much energy on understanding what is entailed in having faith in Jesus that they have failed to ask whether Jesus himself had faith. If it could be established that he did, this would increase our disenchantment of him considerably, with the felicitous result that he would be much more accessible to our experience of trying to live faithful lives. Exegetes, as usual, helped in getting things going in this direction. Something as small as removing the "our" from Hebrews 12:2 opened up new vistas. Most translations of that passage had rendered Jesus as "the pioneer and perfecter of *our* faith," even though the original Greek has no "our." Thus, the New American Bible in its 1988 edition more accurately has Jesus as "the leader and perfecter of faith."[1] This slight change positions Jesus of Nazareth as one who is on our side of the problematic of having to believe what we do not see rather than being on the side of one who sees (the beatific vision) and therefore only seems to be one of us. This comes close to seeing him as having been a rescuer who edifies us but who was not one of us.

In this question about Jesus' faith, it is interesting to note that the last three Vatican-commissioned colloquia on Christology have nowhere claimed that the earthly Jesus possessed the beatific vision.[2] The enchanters, among whom I would have to include St. Thomas Aquinas, would say that "from the first moment of his conception Christ had the full vision of God in his essence . . . therefore he could not have had faith" (*Summa Theologiae* 3, q.7, a.3). But wouldn't this position seem to guarantee that he was never really one of us? We might be able to admire someone like this, but how could you follow him or find out from him what human holiness is? If he already had "the full vision of God" from the first moment of his conception, then he didn't learn the way we learn, and in fact, he would not have had to learn at all. To put it crudely, it makes him seem like a know-it-all who only slowly meted out to others "what the traffic could bear" about his exalted state.

This way of looking at Jesus of Nazareth makes one go back over familiar texts to see them in a new light. If he had faith, for example, what were the objects of his faith? They were the same as Israel's: Israel's election by God; Israel's call to holiness; the divine authority of the law; the coming Messiah; the final reign of God. What is interesting in all of these objects of faith is that Jesus believed each of them. At the same time, the power of his faith was so strong that his understanding of each of these beliefs moves profoundly away from what most of his contemporaries held. By this movement beyond the beliefs that he received, he shows himself a pioneer and a leader of Israel's faith. Take just one example: his belief in the reign of God. That was something Israel had expected for centuries. But Jesus spoke knowingly about its imminence and much more knowingly about its character than any prophet had. But always in similes and parables that were short of direct description because it was still an object of faith for him, not an object of sight. He came to know more about this coming reign than anyone before him, yet he did not speak definitively about it. The fact that he spoke of it in parables suggests that he was not saying the last word on the subject. In fact, with respect to the time of its final arrival, he expressly said he didn't know.

And even when he exhorted his hearers about their need for faith—hoping that it would be at least as big as a mustard seed—and complained to the Twelve about how "little faith" they had and to his audiences about being a faithless generation, he begins to sound like someone who can testify to the power of faith because he had personally experienced the difference between having it and not having it. And his need for getting away from people, to go apart and pray—why would these apparently frequent periods of prayer have been so necessary for him if he was enjoying the direct beatific vision that has been associated with his consciousness for so long?

Jesus' holiness is much more attractive, and he is so much more able to be followed, if he lived a life of faith than if he lived a life of sight. He can be a leader and pioneer and perfecter of our faith if we can see him living a life of faith to the hilt. Take two more examples. The law, first. Jesus' faith did not evolve such that he repudiated Israel's awe about the law. He explicitly indicated that he did not intend "to abolish the law or the prophets," (Matt. 5:17) but he came to a point where he knew the difference between the degree of commitment of the heart these texts were calling for, in contrast to the formal obedience to them he found in much of the leadership of Israel. He came to see that the difference was between a behavioral response to the law and an actual fulfilling of its intent—*with one's whole heart, soul, mind, strength* (Luke 10:27). His was a change not from one faith to another but from one level of insight into Israel's faith to a radically deeper one. Another example: the Messiah. Jesus had inherited an understanding of a Messiah who was going to rid Israel of the scourge of Rome and free Israel from all its enemies. He evolved in his understanding of the Messiah as he himself experienced rejection and scorn, especially from the leadership of Israel. He began to understand the difference between Israel's vaunted image of a conquering, vindicating Messiah and the unsuspected dimensions of the role of a suffering Messiah, which Jesus traced to a deeper reading of the Hebrew Scriptures in the four songs of the suffering servant in Isaiah. Because of the scene on the road to Emmaus, when Jesus tries to explain why he had to suffer (Luke 24), it is easy to imagine him during his ministry poring over the Scriptures

of Israel to try to align his experience of his ever deepening faith
and his being increasingly at odds with the authoritative gate-
keepers of that faith. It was the same faith, but he was taking it to
depths it had not attained before.

Why did his understanding of Israel's objects of faith change
so radically? We might simply say because Jesus practiced it and in
the practice experienced the difference between what he had been
taught to believe and what he found to be true and not true of
those handed-down beliefs. Not that Israel was deceived in its
beliefs—they derived directly from the word of God, but the way
these were construed by his contemporaries did not conform to
the truth as he was coming to see it. Presumably, too, his insight
and judgment were deepening because of the Spirit in a way that
Israel's leadership was not. Which is to say that as Jesus' faith
matured, God had more and more reason to entrust him with the
whole future of belief in God. Jesus' understanding of God and the
ways of God became so trenchant that he would rightly be called
in the last Gospel "the way" (John 14:6). What was he the way to?
To true belief.

In two other matters we can catch glimpses of Jesus' faith
deepening. One of these had to do with his understanding of
Israel's mission. He came to an awareness of Israel's mission and
his special relationship to it. In a number of texts in the Gospels
he is described as astonished at the degree of "faith" he finds in
those outside of Israel. And to his great astonishment he finds that
he is the focus of their faith. They trusted Jesus' relationship with
God, and in some cases, they had greater faith in him than he
found his fellow Israelites had in him. These developments seem
to have changed Jesus' mind about how Israel would be in relation
to the "nations" beyond Israel. Having first thought that he "was
sent only to the lost sheep of the house of Israel" (Matt. 15:24), his
awareness of the scope of his mission was being enlarged. The

enlargement came about because he discovered that God was working in ways and in places and with non-Jews—in a word, much more universally than Jesus' earlier faith had imagined. The more he matured in his understanding of his mission, the more Isaian it became. The prophet Isaiah, especially Third Isaiah, foresaw an Israel whose mission was to the poor, to the captives and their liberty, to the blind and their sight, to the oppressed and their emancipation (Luke 4:18).

The second change is more radical. It has to do with Jesus' growth in perception of the character of God. He became aware of God's nearness and intimate care not only for himself but for the rest of humanity. In some ways this understanding of God is captured in the Lord's Prayer. Perhaps nothing sums up the power of the development of Jesus' faith better than the intimate name "Abba" that he used to personally address the mystery of God. What we don't have in any clear way in the New Testament record is a "before picture," namely, what Jesus' initial understanding of God was. Certainly it was that of Israel as conveyed by the liturgical prayer and psalms of the Hebrew Scriptures, but it also grew into a much more personal relationship with God. His degree of trust in God and intimacy with God is what makes his gospel attractive even now.

How do we explain Jesus' understanding of God? One way is to emphasize the preincarnation ontology: "In the beginning was the Word" (John 1:1). Another way is to emphasize Jesus' growth in faith. The first focuses on Jesus' divinity; the second on his humanity. In the first, Jesus' main task is that of a good teacher, slowly meting out what he fully knows so that his hearers can understand. In the second, his main task is that of a learner, slowly mulling over the texts and his experiences so that he can come to know the God he speaks of with greater and greater clarity.

The Consciousness of Jesus

I believe the better way to address the two issues in the previous section (Jesus' faith and his developing knowledge of God) is by focusing on Jesus' consciousness. We surely have this in common. Specifically, what did Jesus of Nazareth know about God and his own relationship with God, and when did he know it? Getting at what was in Jesus' consciousness is admittedly a perilous inquiry. But we can know something about this. While there are many arcane studies of the consciousness of Jesus, in my mind the best of these is still that of Karl Rahner.[3] Rahner clarifies how Jesus' human consciousness could be united to the second Person of the Blessed Trinity in a hypostatic union and how, at the same time, he could grow in knowledge of both God and himself and of anything else the same way the rest of us do. Rahner does this by examining the many layers of human knowing that operate in all of us. The layer of concepts is only one of these ways. There is more to knowing than simply the explicit knowledge of objects. In fact, something can be known and not known at the same time. Thus, in his consciousness Jesus could know in his early years in some way that he was special to God without having any explicit knowledge of being the Son of God. Rahner shows how ignorance, or not knowing, is not a wholly negative thing but the condition of both freedom and growth in us. Further, Jesus could and did grow in knowledge of God's presence without God ever having become an object "looked at by an observer standing opposite it . . . as if this divine essence were brought into Christ's consciousness from without and occupied this consciousness from without and in all its dimensions and layers"(Ibid., 207).

To say that God was not an object in the human consciousness of Jesus is also to describe my consciousness and yours. God is a presence, a very real presence within a horizon filled with objects of knowledge. God can become a very real presence to us because of who God became for Jesus. Jesus can become an object of knowledge to us because of the degree of God's presence that developed in Jesus' consciousness.

Rahner developed an understanding of the consciousness of Jesus by examining the consciousness of people. In particular, the consciousness of those whom he experienced as holy, among whom was Rahner's own mother. Because of them he could state that "a direct presence to God belongs to the nature of the spiritual person, in the sense of an unsystematic attunement and an unreflected horizon which determines everything else . . . [this is] the permanent basis for all their other spiritual activities . . . [it is] the tacit factor in self-awareness which orders and explains everything but cannot be explained itself" (Ibid., 209).

This is a rich line of reflection that helps to demystify Jesus and bring him into the more common zone of human beings, at least holy human beings. An attunement to God, whose presence within the horizon of one's self-awareness determines all one's activities—this describes the consciousness of the holy person. This attunement grows as one becomes more self-aware and God-aware. I recall a saintly aunt of mine who at the age of ninety-two wondered why she had wasted so much of her life when "all I ever really had to do with my life was to love God." As Rahner put it: "A direct presence to God belongs to the nature of the spiritual person."

Rahner's line of thinking on consciousness does much to preserve the insight of the Council of Chalcedon (451), which declared that the divine and human natures in the one person of Jesus must be understood as having undergone "no confusion, no change, no division, no separation."[4] How then could he have one consciousness? Jesus' knowledge of objects in the world, though distinct from and always qualitatively different from his knowledge of God, was integrated with his knowledge of God, with whom he had "a direct presence," without God being present to him as an object of consciousness. But this is also the way believers know God; there is an unsystematized attunement to that reality. There is also knowledge of God that does not have to come from explicit reflection because God is present within the horizon in which one functions. While this knowledge is unlike the rest of the things we know, it has its roots in them. William Dych comments on Rahner's understanding of consciousness: "Transcendence is not a leap out of the world, but a step by step movement through it. . . . It is only in our encounter with the finite that this transcendence takes place, so that our knowledge of God is always and in every instance mediated by our knowledge of the world."[5]

Understanding Jesus as imbued with the Spirit yet functioning with a human consciousness makes sense of the scriptural scenes that have Jesus clearly questioning, seeking, doubting, learning, being surprised, and even at one point feeling forsaken by God. His responses to what he learned were obviously keener than his contemporaries', since they were undistorted by sin or by the biases that personal sin or sinful cultures generate (otherwise the awed reaction to his person, words, and deeds during his public life is inexplicable). Nonetheless, his consciousness is not functioning from the heights of the beatific vision, as if he were seeing from within the life of the Trinity. This is most evident in his last ordeal. There is no high or descending Christology in the Synoptics' treatment of Jesus' handling of his betrayal, abandonment, torture, mockery, crucifixion, and death. Those texts convey not a figure with "sight" but a figure with the anguish of one who trusted sightlessly—"My God, my God, why have you forsaken me?" (Mark 15:34)—yet one who entrusted himself to the night believing in the nearness and goodness of God. "Holiness not yet" kept flowering into "holiness already" as Jesus came slowly to know and to choose what he needed to know in order to do what

God had chosen him for. A holiness that would circumvent human consciousness *via* a beatific vision would not be a human holiness or a human consciousness. To respond to a call to such a holiness would result in despair.

Jesus' Learning Was Human Learning

Jesus learned the way any human being learns. He learned from others, beginning with those to whom any child accords authority—his parents, his relatives, the faithful members of the synagogue, the available disciplines Israel used for growing in union with God. All of these were essential to his developing his initial identity as a Jew. Would it not have been strange of God to have this Messiah circumvent the ways of growing in knowledge of God that the chosen people had learned over the centuries? His life is best understood as an ascent, a shoot that sprouted from the "stump of Jesse" (Isa. 11:1), not as a descending intruder into the human order from outside of it. His identity and its nurture came from within the people God had called to be his own. A descending mode for his self-understanding could call into question the fairness of God, whose formation of a faithful and holy people had been continual and constant for generations.

Like everything else about the Christian faith, holiness is best understood "from below," by inquiring into Jesus' holiness from his oneness or consubstantiality with our humanity, from his being one of us. Did he think of himself as holy? It's not possible to answer that question, but there are texts that suggest he did not. For example, why did he refuse to accept the compliment from one who called him "good teacher" with "Why do you call me good? No one is good but God alone" (Luke 18:19)? And, more broadly, in his consciousness, was he aware of the limitations of being finite, mortal, ignorant? The New Testament at times depicts Jesus as fully aware of his ignorance. For example, "Of that day or hour [when the heavens and the earth will pass away], no one knows, neither the angels in heaven, nor the Son, but only the Father" (Mark 13:32). Elsewhere he is depicted as limited and a participant in our human weaknesses. "For we do not have a high priest who is unable to sympathize with our weaknesses, but one who has similarly been tested in every way [we are]" (Heb. 4:15).

Using the interpretive lens of the humanity of Jesus, any number of texts begin to look different. So, to go back again to his childhood in Nazareth, he is described as being "obedient" to his mother and father and as having steadily "advanced [in] wisdom and age and favor before God and man" (Luke 2:51–52). In its simplest meaning the text seems to say that as he grew humanly he also grew in holiness. It also suggests that his growth in the virtues was supervised by those who were themselves obedient to the understandings they had from the Hebrew Scriptures and to their Jewish faith. His mother is described (Luke 2:51) as pondering all these things about him in her heart—his sameness with and difference from other conceptions, births, children, circumstances. Is it too much for us to assume that he would have been made privy to her ponderings about what her Jewish faith had taught about holiness and about the Messiah?

From within our own cultural myopia, we too easily see Jesus as a loner who transcended his milieu rather than as someone who heard the call to holiness from those who heard the word of God spoken to Israel and kept it. And even in developing his own unique role in Israel's response to that call, how can we leave out those who were described as markedly moved by God, by an angel, or a dream, or the Spirit? In addition to his mother and his father, what is recorded (and presumably this represents only a

portion of such a group) are stories about Zechariah and Elizabeth, Simeon and Anna. And even when we get beyond this rather
legendary material about his hidden life and into his public life,
there are many places where, through people, we encounter a Jesus
who is intently listening and thereby developing a deeper understanding of himself and of the gospel he teaches.

The Spirit as Teacher

But, of course, to inquire into how Jesus grew in "wisdom, age, and
favor," both as a youth and as a mature man, requires looking at
his relationship with the Holy Spirit. It does not seem to me that
we can attain much light on Jesus' faith or consciousness of God
until we introduce the subject of the Holy Spirit. It is no less true
of Jesus than it is of us that it is "the Spirit [who] scrutinizes everything, even the depths of God" (1 Cor. 2:10). His uniqueness is
best probed by examining his relationship to the Spirit. It was the
Spirit who in stages taught him who he was. His was only a gradual awareness of his uniqueness, not unlike the way the Spirit
teaches Christians their true identities even now. Explaining him
in terms of two natures might have appealed to previous generations, but it is somewhat inaccessible to us. But to see him as the
one person to whom the Spirit had been given "without measure"
(John 3:34, RSV) is not alienating, since this is closer to our traditional understanding of the Spirit and to our experience of ourselves as indwelt by the Spirit, howsoever measured. In brief, he
was a work in progress in holiness, as we are meant to be.

If we think in terms of natures, we can ask the question: How
did the Holy Spirit function in Jesus' human consciousness or
sanctify his human nature? Or we can ask a simpler question: How

did the Holy Spirit function in Jesus' person? Both are valid, but the latter is preferred because it can also enlighten the more universal issue of how people come to truth about themselves and God. Just below the surface in the primary texts we have always had at our disposal, the Gospels and the Epistles, we can see the Spirit functioning in Jesus through a process that reflects the same process by which anyone learns—by experience, observation, insight, judgment, and action. Any human consciousness grows through these ordinary steps to action by plumbing the reality we have access to. The Spirit dwelling in Jesus brought each of these ordinary mental processes to a deeper level, heightening his ability to find God already at work in the people and circumstances that were shaping his self-understanding and mission.

He learned the ways of God the same way he learned the ways of "man" and his world. His experiences flowered into insights as do ours, and his insights matured into judgments as do ours, and his judgments produced choices as do ours, and his choices led him to speak and act as do ours. Like the rest of us, he was on the hunt for what was real, for what was true. Like the rest of us, he was most Godlike when he was pursuing the true and choosing the good. By his growing in consciousness of his own experiencing and perceiving and judging and choosing he was able to come to ever new insight into who he was and what he was called by God to do. The Spirit was able to teach him things about God that were not understood by his contemporaries. So, the parenting character of God was never so deeply appropriated by any of the prophets as it was by Jesus. "Abba," as Jesus' name for God, was the fruit of that listening. And knowing himself both as Son of David and Son of this God was also the fruit. Jesus learned that the concerns of this Abba were about things as little as the hair on his head and as big as "the weightier things of the law:/judgment, and mercy and fidelity" (Matt. 23:23). His growth in consciousness of the truth about God and himself and his mission keeps Jesus from becoming fixated on minutiae. The aspiration to holiness in the Israel into which Jesus was born had often gotten sidetracked in the picayune. In his human consciousness and with his human reason, he was able to discern God at work where others might simply see "flesh" or the mundane or the immediate here and now. His discernment of the ordinary uncovered ever deeper layers of what was true and good. His having housed the Spirit "without reserve" can explain the depth of his consciousness and, therefore, of the judgments he made and choices he arrived at and the holy works that issued from these.

It is obvious from the simple raw data of the Gospels that the human consciousness of Jesus was not being informed about higher math or astrophysics or phenomenology. He didn't grow in factual information that his contemporaries didn't know. What he did grow in was an awareness of the nearness of God to Israel and to him and that this divine presence could be trusted. We put our faith in the faith of Jesus, in particular in his faith that God is utterly trustworthy. We also put our faith in his judgments about himself and his mission as his discernment of his experience of God and humanity evolved.

The Fruit of Listening

The evolution produced in him a maturity about Israel and himself and God. He would, therefore, have believed that God had chosen a people and imbued them with a destiny. He came to know himself as chosen from within Israel's belief that it was chosen. Once he became convinced that the Holy One of Israel had called Israel to become one with God's holiness, he never turned

back from that conviction, though it brought him into confronta-
tions with the compromises of Israel's leadership. Jesus believed
with Isaiah that Israel "shall be called 'My Delight,'/and your land
'Espoused'" (Isa. 62:4). He became conscious of the tenderness of
God by seeing it in the way all creation was cared for, even in the
feeding of birds and the clothing of the wildflowers. Informed by
Joseph's dreams and Mary's words, he was prepared to understand
that as a son of David he had a special role to play in Israel's destiny. Born into a people awaiting the Messiah, he came to understand that he was the Messiah they were awaiting. In all of this
it seems that he came to see who he was to God and to Israel.
But even learning that he was beloved of God, as he apparently
did, did not eradicate from him the radical incomprehensibility
of God.

The kingdom for Jesus was the sovereignty of the holy that
was already beginning in and through his ministry. To enter into
and under this sovereignty did not require that he leave the mundane world nor displace the empirical but that he see these for
what they were. He plumbed the mundane in depth daily till it
yielded its fuller truth. To live in and under the reign of God gave
him a familiarity with God. But this did not entail his circum-
venting the world of experience, and the need for insight, judgment, and action.

Since human beings can't complete themselves by a single
act, he would have had to respond to the Spirit's movements many
times. And he would not have been able to choose what it was he
would be eventually chosen for had he not committed himself all
along the way. But Jesus' ongoing choosing cannot be explained
except by the growing bond of love that developed with the One
who chose him. In all the other things that have been said about
Jesus, love is at the core of the explanation of his life. The Spirit
was the source both of his growth in personal truth and his

growth in love. It was the Spirit that had come to rest on him at his baptism that explains his choosing to love with a constancy that mirrored God's own constancy and love. But love is like a seed, which when planted needs to grow. Its growth is measurable by acts of love. In Jesus, this love had the added dimension of the reign of God come into time and history.

If we were to speak of the agenda of the indwelling Spirit in Jesus of Nazareth, it would seem to be that it was for his learning the truth about God, himself, Israel, his mission. But, of course, he had to love the truth he learned and do the truth he learned to love. It was in this that his special relationship with God became manifest. There is a troika here that appears to be inextricable: holiness, truth, and love. But when one inquires about the Spirit's agenda for Israel and the followers of Jesus, the same troika seems to apply. The Holy Spirit is the Spirit of truth and of love. Where the Spirit is, there truth and love are. Holiness grows where truth and love are. If Jesus had stopped asking questions, truth would have become static. Truth grows with questions pursued and answered. There wasn't another way if he really was one of us. And it is the same with love: it grows or doesn't grow depending on whether one acts on the good one knows to be true.

The reign of God, or the sovereignty of the holy, has laws of development to be obeyed just as consciousness has. Jesus' parables convey his understanding of those "laws." From a few of his parables, one could conclude that one of the laws of the reign of God was the need to detect it notwithstanding its almost imperceptible beginnings. Another law was that it needed room to grow to become what it was meant to become. Its growth is on its terms, not on the terms of the soil in which it takes root. Another law is that the recipient never presumes to be the source of it but is wholly beholden and dependent on it. To put these three laws in Jesus' words: "This is how it is with the kingdom of God. . . . a man were to scatter seed on the land and would sleep and rise night and day and the seed would sprout and grow, he knows not how. Of its own accord the land yields fruit, first the blade, then the ear, then the full grain in the ear" (Mark 4:26–28). Jesus was describing the effects on himself of yielding to the Spirit in himself and on those to whom he ministered. The beginnings were usually as small as a seed sown by the Sower, but the fullness that was to come was already there in promise if the seed were given room. Eventually he understood that things of the kingdom and the agenda of the Spirit were one and the same. He came to see that these seeds bridged time with eternity. Then he came to see that he himself had an unprecedented role to play in detecting and inaugurating that reign in history.

The Spirit of Jesus

I have been pushing a "low Christology" in all of the above in order to connect Jesus' holiness with our own and to find him to be the icon of holiness for our humanity. This will not sit well with those who know only a "high Christology." Of course a high Christology is valid, true, and warranted, but it is best seen as having developed incrementally. In other words, the naming of the reality of Jesus develops during his ministry and does not stop with his resurrection and ascension. Rather, it deepens exponentially with the descent of the Spirit upon the community. It is only then that Jesus comes to be named by more and more exalted titles, such as Lord and Savior, and more and more stupefying claims such as "image of the invisible God" in whom "were created all things in heaven and on earth" (Col. 1:15–16). Add the creeds and the christological councils, and one would have to conclude that this evolution in the understanding of who Jesus was makes no sense at all unless the same Spirit that taught Jesus who he was also taught the community the full truth of his identity. The Spirit was sent by the Father and the Son to lead Jesus' followers "to all truth" (John 16:13), especially truth about him and his mission and themselves and their part in this mission. Otherwise, the postresurrection community was guilty of illusion or idolatry.

We rightly name and praise Jesus as Lord because of the gift we have received of the Holy Spirit (1 Cor. 12:3). But in doing so we might have lost sight of him as also our brother. The same Spirit would teach us this just as surely as we have been taught that he is Lord. If we lose this one-of-us way of seeing and naming him, our praise will be lavished on one who has been transcendentalized and separated from the people through whom he came to understand who he was. Our homage does not do Jesus justice if we raise him so far above the human order that he exits it. And it does not do us justice if we lose sight of the divinity we each have because of Jesus. This, of course, will make no sense unless the Spirit is the source of the transformation of consciousness in both Jesus and us, about us and him. Further, the Holy Spirit is at the center of the sameness we have with Jesus in this matter of holiness. Jesus' holiness had the same source as ours now has.

When did Jesus have a consciousness of his divinity? This is the same question we had at the beginning of the chapter: What did he know about himself, and when did he know it? According to the Gospels of John and Luke one could claim that he should have known his pedigree as soon as he came to consciousness. For example, wouldn't his mother have told him what the angel told her? "The holy Spirit will come upon you, and the power of the Most High will overshadow you. Therefore the child to be born will be called holy, the Son of God" (Luke 1:35). But the New Testament and the Gospels in particular were written after the fact, after the Spirit had taught the community the full truth about Jesus of Nazareth. Now that we know that, our spirituality should appropriate the significance. We must, in other words, have a low Christology if we are to appreciate what it took for Jesus to warrant the high christological understandings we rightly have of him now. "He had to become like his brothers [and sisters] in every way, that he might be a merciful and faithful high priest before God, to expiate the sins of the people" (Heb. 2:17).

If he is like us in every way, then it is legitimate to ask about the connection between his having been conceived by the Holy Spirit and those of us who have been "born from above of water and the Spirit" at some point after our conceptions. Sacramentally we, his baptized-in-the-Spirit followers, have the same source and kind of holiness that he had; both he and we have been born from above. Is our having been adopted as children of God rather than born God's children a reason to ignore or disparage the dignity of our condition?

The Truing Spirit

What I have tried to do in this chapter so far is to show how to make Jesus an icon of human holiness by examining his faith and his human consciousness. We will now return to the material of the second chapter and see how he came to embody in his person the strands of holiness that were left unconnected in Israel's many comprehensions of it. Seeing this process at work in him enables us to re-enchant holiness.

But in order to do this the reader must suffer a term and an idea about the Spirit that is not ordinary. When I get away from all the texts and considerations about Jesus' consciousness and his faith, I am prompted to ask a simple question: How did the Spirit make Jesus special, the icon of human holiness? I see the Spirit as the One who *trues* Jesus. The English language seldom uses *true* as a verb anymore. It did in earlier generations, usually in connection with constructing things. So a wall or lumber or a tool can be trued, meaning that it is made to balance, or it is leveled to fit, or squared or made even, or brought to the right length or up to specification. It takes a truer to true, and the material to be trued, and a design in the mind of the truer. What is trued must be pliable for a truer to fashion it for the part it is meant to play in the overall design of what is being constructed.

All of these aspects of truing seem to fit the person of Jesus. The Spirit was the Truer of Jesus. The Spirit gently crafted the identity of Jesus and accompanied him as he carried out all that God had intended. Specifically, Jesus needed the gifts of wisdom, understanding, knowledge, and counsel to meet the challenges of having the new creation emerge from the old. The Spirit's accompaniment of Jesus can be described by saying that the Spirit trued him, deftly bending each aspect of his humanity to do and become that for which he was sent. When his will flagged or recoiled, the gifts of courage, fear of the Lord, and piety stabilized him or trued him so that he could become the instrument God needed for the salvation of the world. What Jesus needed were great gifts of both intellect and will, which, according to the church, is what the gifts of the Spirit effect in the rest of us. In a word, the gifts of the Spirit trued him to be about the mission God intended for him to accomplish.

More specifically, it would appear that the primary means the Spirit used to true the heart and mind of Jesus was the word of God. The Scriptures themselves, without the gifts, even the devil knows and quotes. But Jesus was trued by the word of God because the Spirit mentored him in their meaning. Truing today is done the same way with gifts and the word of God taught by the same Truer. The Spirit of truth trued Jesus, fashioning him according to the design that God intended. The beginnings of that design we have seen in the second chapter and the strands of holiness the Scriptures revealed. Their correct understanding sometimes necessitated wisdom, sometimes counsel, sometimes knowledge, sometimes understanding. And the Spirit of love trued him by giving him a fear of the Lord that enabled him to be constantly in awe of God at work in the surroundings he both touched and was touched by. It gave him the courage to carry out the paradoxical role the suffering Messiah was called to perform, and it gave him the piety to be in a relationship of such familiarity with God that he could credibly proclaim the loving-kindness of his God and ours.

Subsuming the Strands

The six understandings of holiness elaborated in the previous chapter came to be interpreted by Jesus and the early church as subsumed by him so that the six became one in his person.

GENESIS

The main features of the story of the origin of creation are appropriated by and subsumed into him. He clearly functions within a horizon that savors the goodness of every part of creation and sees each part under the benevolent providence of the Creator. Where another would see only the birds of the air and the lilies of the field, he sees them being fed and clothed by God.

Jesus also begins to look like a new Adam who obeyed the command of God to Adam to "have dominion" over what God had created (Gen. 1:26). In fact, his dominion over nature becomes a source of astonishment to his disciples. "Who then is this whom even [the] wind and sea obey?" they asked as they saw him at times transcend the laws of nature (Mark 4:41).

But Jesus also begins to subsume in himself the story of origin in Genesis in several ways. He was Sabbath observant; he was not Sabbath subservient. When it seemed necessary, he healed on the Sabbath because resting in God and overcoming all alienation from God was the point of the Sabbath. By his own Sabbath observance and by his observance of Israel's liturgical discipline (up to and including the Passover meal the night before he died), he was understood to have subsumed the import of Sabbath into himself. "Come to me . . . and you will find rest for yourselves" (Matt. 11:28–29). The function of the holy day in Israel came to be housed in Jesus and its legalism transcended.

The Abraham story is another piece in the Genesis account of holiness that becomes subsumed into the Gospel account of who Jesus was. In the debate between Jesus and "the Jews" on the issue of who they were (John 8), Jesus denies that Abraham is their father because they do not believe the truth he speaks about himself. He is saying that Abraham's believing, his own believing, and the believing of his hearers must be all of a piece for each of the three parties to be right with God. "Whoever belongs to God hears the words of God; for this reason you do not listen, because you do not belong to God" (John 8:47). Then the high Christology of the Gospel of John is evident: "[I solemnly declare it:] before Abraham came to be, I AM" (John 8:58). If all the communities of the earth were to find a blessing in Abraham, that blessing was now being declared as actually coming from the "I AM" who preceded Abraham. The blessing of being right with God now has a new medium.

Exodus

Moses is the central figure in the book of Exodus. Under Moses, Israel came together as a nation and was given the Sinai teachings that would have Israel cohere as a people who would be pleasing to God. Jesus is the new Moses; in the Gospel of Matthew he is explicitly portrayed in this way. The new Moses has authoritative emendations ("But I say to you . . .") to add to the law that Moses carried down on tablets from Mount Sinai, which are to be obeyed in the heart. The righteousness of the law bears the fruit of holiness in the new law.

Even more obvious is the exodus this new Moses preached and then embodied with the gift of his life. By being crucified, only to be raised up by his Father so that those who put their faith in him could come to the land of direct participation in the life of God, this new Moses is the forerunner of this new condition. Like Jesus, the follower would have to lose his or her life to find it. This new land is not without the discipline of the law, but it is a discipline of the heart as interpreted by one who had a face-to-face familiarity with God, as Moses had. Jesus leads into freedom those who have faith in his faith by inviting them to "take my yoke upon you and learn from me. . . . For my yoke is easy, and my burden light" (Matt. 11:29–30). By his self-offering, holiness becomes a possibility for many and a reality for those who accept his summons to adhere to him in faith.

Deuteronomy

No one had been clasped by God's embrace more fully than Jesus of Nazareth. From the number of citations of the book of Deuteronomy in the synoptic Gospels it seems this book pervasively shaped Jesus' consciousness. One brief example: immediately

before his public ministry Jesus is led into the wilderness "by the
Spirit . . . to be tempted by the devil" (Matt. 4:1). After fasting
for forty days and forty nights, he refuses the blandishments of
all three temptations by quoting Deuteronomy. He turns back
the first by telling the devil that one does not live by bread alone
"but by every word that comes forth from the mouth of the
LORD" (Deut. 8:3); the second temptation, by deflecting the lure
of self-display of casting himself down from the pinnacle of the
temple, with "You shall not put the LORD, your God, to the test"
(Deut. 6:16); and the third temptation, by refusing the deal the
devil is trying to strike of sharing homage: "The LORD, your
God, shall you fear; him shall you serve" (Deut. 6:13). Jesus' loyalty is being put to the test before he begins his ministry.
Covenant loyalty is the main theme of Deuteronomy, and
Matthew's Jesus shows himself true to its understanding of loyalty. Jesus is being presented as the loyal Son of God. Unlike
Israel, who, as God's son (Deut. 1:31; 14:1; 32:5–6), failed the
test in the wilderness, Jesus passes it.

Here, as elsewhere in the New Testament, the portrait painted
is of a Jesus who perfectly fulfilled the stipulations that Israel was
called to. Israel had been chosen to be a people for the Lord's own
possession "because the LORD loved you" (Deut. 7:8). God "keeps
his merciful covenant down to the thousandth generation toward
those who will love him and keep his commandments" (Deut. 7:9).
Jesus lived his life within the covenant embrace that Israel had been
invited into by God. In Deuteronomy, God's covenant initiative
was completed by the human response of love. But as in the previous two sections, there is a subsuming into Jesus of this central
theme. Deuteronomic holiness is attained and superseded at the
Last Supper with Jesus' "this cup is the new covenant in my blood,
which will be shed for you" (Luke 22:20).

EZEKIEL

This prophet conveyed the holiness of God's name to an exiled Israel. His message was that the divine name separated Israel from the profane; Israel was chosen to be the dwelling place for his name. But because Israel was so negligent about separating itself from the profane, the Divine Name was never at rest where it had chosen to rest because of Israel's hard-heartedness. But rather than withdraw from Israel, Ezekiel has God making a preposterous promise: to remove its unfaithful heart and "give you a new heart and place a new spirit within you" (Ezek. 36:26). This prophecy was fulfilled in Jesus. In him God's name found a place to rest. So fully did the Divine Name come to rest in Jesus of Nazareth that "God greatly exalted him/and bestowed on him the name/that is above every name/. . . Jesus Christ is Lord" (Phil. 2:9–11).

Lord is English for the Greek *kyrios,* which, in turn, renders the ineffable name of *Yhwh,* Yahweh, the Hebrew name for God. But Jesus' lordship is so exalted that it extends over the whole universe. This name, which is above every other name, is bestowed on Jesus by God, because "he humbled himself,/becoming obedient to death,/even death on a cross" (Phil. 2:8). As a result of this bestowal "at the name of Jesus/every knee should bend,/of those in heaven and on earth and under the earth" (Phil. 2:10). This is an amazing thing for God to do. Jesus of Nazareth is now made Lord and is to be so named and given homage over the three realms over which God alone was sovereign. "Every knee" must bend to this decision of God, and rather than diminishing God's glory, all of this is "to the glory of God the Father" (Phil. 2:11).

This hymn in the letter to the Philippians can be connected to the Last Supper discourse in the Gospel of John, where Jesus, facing his final humiliation, prays: "Father, glorify your name" (John 12:28). "I glorified you on earth by accomplishing the work that you gave me to do. Now glorify me, Father, with you, with the glory that I had with you before the world began. I revealed your name to those whom you gave me out of the world" (John 17:4–6). Under the motif of name we have further evidence of the New Testament's subsuming still another holiness theme of the Hebrew Scriptures.

ISAIAH

Jesus was no less aware of the holiness of God than Isaiah was. He was equally aware that he lived with people of unclean lips. He would have appropriated Isaiah's understanding of the source of the Messiah's exceptionality: that the Spirit of the Lord was to rest upon the successor to David and he would be imbued with the gifts of the Spirit: "a spirit of wisdom and of understanding,/A spirit of counsel and of strength,/a spirit of knowledge and of fear of the LORD" (Isa. 11:2). As these gifts developed and became more manifest in Jesus, his ministry flourished and at the same time became a cause of division for those who, moved by a different spirit, determined to kill him.

Isaiah is the text used by Jesus to inaugurate his public ministry. Jesus, having returned to Nazareth and its synagogue, is handed the scroll of Isaiah and reads: "The Spirit of the Lord is upon me,/because he has anointed me/to bring glad tidings to the poor./He has sent me to proclaim liberty to captives/and recovery of sight to the blind,/to let oppressed go free,/and to proclaim a year acceptable to the Lord" (Luke 4:18–19). He then proceeds to connect this passage to his own person: "Today this scripture passage is fulfilled in your hearing" (Luke 4:21). He is envisioning his ministry exactly in Isaian terms. The poor, the captives, the maimed, those who were imprisoned for debt, all absorbed his attention. It was to these that glad tidings were announced. Jesus'

ministry was to succeed with such as these and fail with those for
whom Isaiah's justice theme was not acceptable.

The last part of Isaiah, with its emphasis on the marginal, is
also a theme in Jesus' message. "When you hold a banquet, invite
the poor, the crippled, the lame, the blind. . . . For you will be
repaid at the resurrection of the righteous" (Luke 14:13–14).
Immediately following this Isaian justice-holiness theme is a para-
ble in which the preoccupied refuse the invitation to the lavish
banquet thrown for them, and in their stead it is attended by those
who are gathered up from the streets and alleys of the town, "the
poor and the crippled, the blind, and the lame" (Luke 14:21).
Those who owned something were too easily owned by it; those
who owned nothing were ready to respond to the invitation. The
Isaian prophecies about the poor, about universality and about
inclusion in First, Second, and Third Isaiah respectively, were subsumed into the ministry and message of Jesus.

It seems likely that the four servant songs of Isaiah were
essential to Jesus' understanding of the seeming failure of his ministry. Especially in the last of these songs, the holiness and the suffering of the servant is brought into a single picture. "It was our
infirmities that he bore,/our sufferings that he endured,/While we
thought of him as stricken,/as one smitten by God and afflicted"
(Isa. 53:4). Why was he so afflicted? "He was pierced for our
offenses,/crushed for our sins. . . ./We had all gone astray like
sheep,/each following his own way;/But the LORD laid upon him/
the guilt of us all" (Isa. 53:5–6). What was the consequence of his
submission of himself like a lamb led to the slaughter? "He shall
take away the sins of many,/and win pardon for their offenses"
(Isa. 53:12). If "he made him to be sin who did not know sin, so
that we might become the [holiness] of God" (2 Cor. 5:21), then
his suffering and our holiness are eternally linked.

JOB

It is easy to overlook the Joblikeness of Jesus; that in his ministry he suffers, anguishes, is tortured in his soul almost to the point of expiring under the weight. "My soul is sorrowful even to death," he says to Peter, James, and John in the Garden of Gethsemane (Mark 14:34). In all of this he is Joblike and learns to submit his own suffering to the reign of God, leaving God free to be God for him and for us. He and his holiness are re-enchanted for us if we know that his suffering was real. He was willing to submit himself to what he does not see but trusts that God does. "Abba [O Father], all things are possible to you. Take this cup away from me, but not what I will but what you will" (Mark 14:36). Job ends up with an act of complete faith saying to the Lord: "I know that you can do all things,/and that no purpose of yours can be hindered" (Job 42:2). In both Jesus and Job there is an entrustment of themselves to what they can neither see nor understand. The description of faith from Hebrews fits the consciousness of Jesus and Job: "Faith is the realization of what is hoped for and evidence of things not seen" (Heb. 11:1).

Sin was the backdrop of the conundrum about suffering in the book of Job. Why, since he was pronounced to be a person of such integrity by God, did he have to suffer? Sin is the backdrop of the conundrum in Jesus' suffering. Why, if he was without sin, did he have to suffer? Although Job's and Jesus' sufferings are not a complete parallel, of course, sin is the reason why there is suffering and death even though the sin is not committed by either of the sufferers, as in this case. The only logic that can be brought to the question of suffering and death is the logic of the cross. Job would not have known this; Jesus learned it at the cost of his life.

The Authority of Holiness

I will end this chapter by connecting two things that now seem right to connect: Jesus' authority and his holiness. There are so many layers to Christology, from the low to the high, that the simple connection between Jesus as holy and his authority can be missed. Or, as is more usual, his authority is located in ontological categories that are somewhat foreign to the modern mind. But Peter in the first catechesis did not miss the connection. He explained the Pentecost event to the astonished onlookers by underscoring his understanding of this connection. To the crowd trying to make sense of the scene, Peter explained that "after the baptism that John preached, how God anointed Jesus of Nazareth with the holy Spirit and power. He went about doing good" (Acts 10:37–38). His authority, his power, came from his anointing by the Holy Spirit. The authority of holiness does not end there or with Jesus alone. "The Fathers of the Church understood that it is from the fullness of the Holy Spirit of Jesus that we have and received and [still] receive grace upon grace! In him, bodily, dwells all the fullness of the Holy Spirit and in him we share in this fullness."[6] From his baptism in the Jordan on, holiness and authority have a Christic stamp that was not there before that event. Henceforth, the Spirit will sanctify and imbue others with the authority of holiness according to the pattern established by Jesus.

I think that we can best glimpse this connection in the beginning of the Gospel of Mark, where Jesus begins to "astonish" and "amaze" his fellow Israelites. Unlike the other three Gospels, which had already introduced Jesus in terms of his ontological specialness—Matthew and Luke in their birth accounts and John in the Prologue—Mark has no introduction to describe Jesus' difference until John baptizes him: "On coming up out of the water he saw the heavens being torn open and the Spirit, like a dove, descending upon him" (Mark 1:10). The consequences of this anointing can be seen in all the subsequent scenes that convey Jesus' enormous authority. First of all Jesus is victorious over the blandishments of Satan, who tested him in the wasteland for forty days. Then he shows the power of his holiness by winning those whom he calls: Simon and Andrew, who immediately "left their nets and followed him" (Mark 1:18), then James and John, who abandoned their father to follow Jesus just as abruptly as the previous two. Next, he enters the synagogue at Capernaum and holds the people "astonished at his teaching" (Mark 1:22). His teaching differed from that of the scribes because of the source of its authority. That of the scribes was their knowledge of the Scriptures. What was this authority that Jesus was exercising that could command the realm of hearts and of minds and of Satan? It was the authority of holiness. The authority of the holiness of God had come to rest on a human being.

As if to underscore the scope of this authority, Mark immediately introduces the man in the synagogue with the unclean spirit who is in such pain in the presence of this holiness that he shrieks: "What have you to do with us, Jesus of Nazareth? Have you come to destroy us? I know who you are—the Holy One of God!" The clash between unholiness and holiness is dramatic. Jesus rebukes the unclean spirit sharply: "Quiet! Come out of him." And after convulsing the man violently, the spirit comes out of him "with a loud cry" (Mark 1:23–26). Most likely the people knew the man, because Capernaum was a small town, and it is also likely that he was a regular member of the synagogue. This would explain why the people acted as they did—with amazement. "What is this? A new teaching with authority. He commands even the unclean spirits and they obey him" (Mark 1:27). His was an authority over and the antithesis to unholiness.

As the Gospel of Mark unfolds, Jesus forgives sins, heals, and restores humans to being right with God. In the second chapter of Mark, in the pericope about the paralytic lowered from the roof of the home in which Jesus was teaching, the paralytic's sins are forgiven. The scribes in attendance, who have never known this kind of authority, are horrified, since only God has power over the realm of sin. Knowing that they judged him to be blaspheming, he lets the whole crowd know that he has "authority on earth to forgive sins" by healing the body of the man whose soul he has just cleansed.

Peter could speak personally about the power of Jesus' holiness. The Gospel of John ends with a scene that reinforces the beginning scenes of Mark. Jesus reminds Peter that "'when you were younger, you used to dress yourself and go where you wanted; but when you grow old, you will stretch out your hands, and someone else will dress you and lead you where you do not want to go.' He said this signifying by what kind of death he would glorify God" (John 21:18–19). This enigmatic *someone else* is the most interesting term here. This *someone else* who will catch Peter up and take him where he would not otherwise go is the Spirit. Jesus' comment to Peter could well be autobiographical because it perfectly fits the experience of Jesus before and after his baptism. Before that he went about as he pleased. After his baptism he is tethered, in a manner of speaking, to the Spirit and its promptings to go in directions he would never have chosen were he on his own. The otherwise unnamed *"someone else"* who would tie him fast is clearly the Spirit in several of the other places in John's Gospel. Certainly in this discourse with Peter, which is recorded as taking place after Passion, Crucifixion, and Resurrection, Jesus would not have had any doubts that his own ministry was a "kind of death [by which] he would glorify God." And since Pentecost had already taken place in John's Gospel on Easter night, without knowing it, Peter was already tethered to the Spirit in this post-Easter scene on the shore of the Sea of Tiberias. Now the momentous transfer can take place. When Jesus had finished speaking he said to Peter, "Follow me." (John 21:19). In other words, now that Peter has given evidence that the Spirit had been truing him by these three avowals of love of Jesus, Jesus invites him to "follow me" into the unknown, being led by the Spirit, that he too might glorify God by losing his life and finding it as he did.

Knowing and saying the truth the Spirit had taught him cost Jesus his life and glorified God. This was to be no less true of Peter. The risen Jesus, now back in the mystery of the Trinity from which he had come, is now seen as assisting the Spirit in stretching Peter by wresting this triple confession of love from him and then commissioning him to tend the sheep Jesus had died for. The holiness of authority is now passed from Jesus to Peter. But Jesus remains preeminently the one through whom the holiness of authority would be forthcoming. He was the cornerstone who was rejected by the builders only to find himself quarried to support a building of living stones that were to house the holiness of God in time and space. Living stones support those around them. Together they are making a dwelling place for God.

4

In Search of the Good

WE HAVE JUST DISCUSSED the uniqueness of Jesus, but what about his followers? Why does one desire to follow him and another not? Desire is an important component of our subject. I will begin this chapter introspectively, saying some things about myself as a desiring self. If Descartes can get away with "I think, therefore I am," I should be given the same chance for an assertion of equal profundity: "I desire, therefore I am incomplete." I act on my desires all the day long. Most of them are innocuous: I answer the phone because I desire to know who is calling; I pick up the papers on the floor because I want the expected student to think I am neater than I am; I turn on the radio for scores, hoping against hope that my team has won. Listing these trivia could be endless since *desirous* is probably the truest adjective I could use about myself. Or, put negatively, I'm never satisfied.

After examining the anatomy of my desires I would conclude that they all have this in common: my desires are always for something that appears to be good. I have a hard time imagining any action I take that is not prompted by some desire. And I have a hard time imagining a desire that doesn't have some seeming good prompting it. We deal with being incomplete by being ever on the move toward becoming more complete by what we conjure as a series of goods, which then we seek to possess or know or consume or become. Another thing this simple introspection uncovers is that these desires are not of equal weight. I have large, long-term desires, for example, writing this chapter and finishing this book, and small, short-term desires such as getting more heat in this room. Some desires are needs and are immediate; other desires are purposes or goals or ends. Yet it is also the case that not all my desires are right to act on—in fact, some are in conflict! The good is sometimes only seeming. Conflicted, I must forgo acting on some desires in order to be able to act on others. I must decide which of these conflicting desires is the better to act on, or more true to myself, and more aligned with my overall sense of purpose.

The Nature of Desire

Purpose and desire connect. Purposes are large desires; desires are small purposes. All of my desires and my purposes are born of my incompleteness: they are all attempts at completing me. Early in my life I traded a desire for an unreal holiness for a desire to be simply real and, therefore, to know more and more about what was/is real or, more precisely, what was/is true. The real and the true were good, truly good. However, the knowledge of the real or true was not something I wanted to contemplate for itself, but to take action on and to live a life in the light of them. This unsophisticated anthropology, conveyed by this brief reflection, makes me think that knowing what is good and desiring it enables me to become "all that I can be," to paraphrase the U.S. Army slogan. However, desire in itself is not good, and I have already stated that my desires and goals conflict. How do I—or any of us—figure out which of these desires is the better one, the one that will preserve some sense of integrity?

Running alongside the sorting out of desires in my life is still another purpose. It has to do with the desire I have always had to share everything that goes on in me with someone and to be both understood and accepted by that other who has the same desire I have. This is one reason people get married, I presume. I didn't, but I can indulge a fantasy about this imagined other. I really want this idealized other to be able to lead me further in the directions my desires go—into deeper and deeper insight into what is true and good, way beyond my own mind's perceptivity and will's tenacity. This desired, idealized other is admittedly larger than life. I am also aware of needing this other to be so far ahead of me in these two directions of the true and the good that I would be following this other in these, and yet treated as an equal in what we have in common by way of desires. This would be a soul mate, you could say, or a perfect partner or a priceless companion. Our mutuality would be such that our desires for "the more" and their attainment would complement each other. In fact, many new desires would come from my relationship with this imagined perfect mate who would be like me in all the things mentioned here, yet unlike me in the limitations I find in myself and have found in imperfect others, with respect to having and meeting these desires for more of the true and the good. Our oneness would be so satisfying that "me" would have become "we," so knowledgeable, trustworthy, lovable, and good would that fantasized perfect partner be.

The more I reflect on this very real desire for a perfect companion, the more I become aware that it has one other important feature to it. I imagine that this partner and I are wholly invested in something much larger than ourselves and our relationship, something that is all-consuming and worthy of our total investment. I want to do something with my life, something that is worth giving my life to, that will redound to the quality of life for others. Only as it unfolds will I learn what the shape and finality of this life-consuming project will be. Since I don't have this depth of vision myself, my companion will have to see more deeply into it than I do and lead the way as we seek to actualize this depth of vision of the good, this larger-than-my-life dream. I will come back to this desire later in this chapter.

Ignatius Loyola

One saint/man who had a genius for figuring out this aspect of his humanity and ours is Ignatius Loyola. For the most part, the first twenty-six years of his life were spent pursuing his desires for what he referred to as his own glory. This took the form of wanting to win the attention of some women in his society. He craved their attention and adulation and, it seems at times, their sexual favors. He was not a womanizer, though he was thought to have fathered a child. His peculiar kind of lust was for attention, reputation, the credit of a great name on earth gained by being known for valiant military feats—in a word, glory. There was a suffocating self-centeredness in these desires. The cannonball that shattered his leg at Pamplona began a conversion process that has made him into what I believe is Western civilization's master for discerning desires.[1]

Laid up and immobilized in his brother's castle at Loyola in the Basque region of Spain, Ignatius became aware of the moral, and a kind of religious schizophrenia that had marked his personality and life up to that point. In effect he realized "I live disconnectedly; there are at least two 'me's' at war with one another." These were two levels of desire in him. The more active and virtually all-encompassing one was for honor/glory. The second tier, his layer of beliefs, was affectively and effectively inactive. Remote from his consciousness, landlocked within his sleeping faith, was a very faint call to holiness. What laid bare his moral and religious schizophrenia was the reflection he undertook on his desire patterns in his very slow convalescence. One of these was a romance pattern that was still very narcissistic—he desired to be avidly admired by a particular woman higher in rank than a countess or duchess. These imaginings led to hours of reverie in which he himself was the paramour, while the one beholding his gallantry and prowess would grow bewitched by him. His imaginings satisfied him vicariously. For those moments he was someone extraordinarily special and an object of adulation to the aristocratic lady whose identity he never revealed.

The second layer of desire, which was still almost completely moribund, began to stir when the only remedy he had for his utter boredom was to read from a book that was in the castle, about the lives of the saints. Remember, he was almost completely immobilized. His experience of reading these pious stories began to work on his fecund imagination. He found himself daydreaming about what it would be like to be in the shoes of one of these saints. He began to imagine "I could be like Dominic or Francis." Then he imagined himself imitating some of their extraordinary feats. He found himself peaceful after these reveries, whereas he came to realize how agitated he was after the reveries about being a lover. This difference really caught his attention.

The lives of these saints were his beliefs fully lived! They stirred up and embodied a deep, though still faint, desire in him to live a holy life. He wasn't becoming a multiple personality or abandoning his own personality to become someone else. Rather, the saints' lives informed him about who he already was at the level of his beliefs, but these beliefs had never become desires and convictions driving him to live a holy life. He had always known the Jesus story, but these saints had followed it without reserve. The Jesus story was one of Ignatius's stories but not the one he was invested in. It had elicited virtually no desires in him. The question he began to ask himself was: If the Gospel became my organizing story, would I be happy? If Christ became my organizing desire, the love I organized my life around, would I be happy? When in his imagination he followed his customary desires, he found he was out of sorts, "dry and dissatisfied." But when he imagined following Jesus, as the saints had, he was peaceful and joyful. This is how his conversion began.

The psychology operating here is worth pausing over. His preaccident desires did not include any noticeable desire for holiness. His religious beliefs lay below the surface eliciting little attention. He accepted the truth of these beliefs because he had neither reason to doubt their truth nor any interest in testing them. His beliefs were lodged in what Thomas Aquinas would call his "passive intellect." But truth is not yet truth until the active intellect takes what the passive intellect presents to it and judges it to be true or not true.[2] Without transferring his beliefs from his passive to his active intellect, Ignatius remained two-tiered. His narcissistic desires continued to drive him while his religious beliefs below these neither energized him nor gave him direction. He attended to those desires that were for his own glory. They propelled him. It's not that he did not perform the practices of the Catholic faith. He did, but not as one who acted from them with the conviction and ardor called for. Whenever the disparity between his desires and his beliefs became too great, he confessed his sins so that he could regain a sense of his still very superficial integrity.

A belief must be personally appropriated as true for it to become operative and a source of energy *in the believer.* Jesus' consubstantiality with his Father's divinity is a case in point. If the "is true" is not personally appropriated, the belief has not yet been made mine. But even when the intellect accepts the truth, it is only partly mine. It becomes wholly mine when it becomes a good of the will since when this happens it begins to elicit desires. Action is taken because this truth *is* now seen as good *for me,* truth *for me.* When the will sees good in what the intellect says is true, desire is mature.

Once the truths of his faith came alive, it seems Ignatius couldn't get enough of God. Mass, penance, devotions, the hours, confession, pilgrimages—there was no end to his activity. This was not spiritual gluttony, however. Rather, his autobiography details the story of a man whose passionate desire was moving from seeking honor for himself to learning to desire and live for the honor and glory of God.

There is much wisdom about discernment in Ignatius which has been useful for many for almost five centuries. But even more foundational is getting the truths of the faith to become my truth, my good, so that they spawn the holy desires that move my life. Then, there's the active desire pattern that will need to be discerned. In the first chapter I examined holiness ontologically, that is, from the point of view of the redemptive character of Jesus' self-immolation. Here I am examining holiness psychologically or as a desirable way of living one's life. A holy life is organized around truth loved and around the One from whom all truth comes and to whom all loved truth leads. When true beliefs become convictions and convictions become wellsprings of action, a holy life can become a reality, psychologically. The best-kept secret to holiness of life is having holy desires. But the Spirit ordinarily gifts us with holy desires through the faculties God has given us: the intellect and will.

Another Abraham

Ignatius was another Abraham and, like Abraham, a nomad. As a nomad he went from one good to another, seeking to meet his own and his family's needs. Then came the call and his response to the call, which was to place his faith in the One calling. Acting in faith, he ceased to be a nomad and became a pilgrim. A pilgrim is going somewhere while a nomad is going round and round, nowhere in particular. Each is pursuing a good. The nomad's goods are ad hoc; the pilgrim's goods are seen as good in light of the pilgim's destination.

We can trace a jump start in the maturity of humanity in the brief accounts of Abraham. It is maturity in the direction of freedom and holiness. Of freedom, because immediate gratification could be postponed, and long-term purposes, intending a longer-term good, could gradually be pursued. Of holiness, because of a telltale line about Abraham in Genesis 15:6, that is, "Abram put his faith in the LORD, who credited it to him as an act of righteousness." Something startling and new enters human history with Abraham's believing. This new ingredient is righteousness. Righteousness is being right with God. Being right with God is a pre-Christ kind of holiness. Humanity's being right with God was to be the ultimate purpose of sending the Son into the world. Being right with God is the consequence of the redeeming act of Christ. Abraham's righteousness anticipates the holiness of God won for us in Christ. Abraham's faith was an augur of our condition as a redeemed people. The plan begins to unfold with Abraham, since the promise to him is that "your descendants [will be] as countless as the stars of the sky and the sands of the seashore" (Gen. 22:17). It is all the difference in the world whether one is a descendant of this mythic figure or not, the difference being that one can be counted among the blessed by God or among the still-to-be counted. Ignatius not only knew the story of Abraham, he replicated it.

Abrahamic holiness develops out of a response to a call; it lives in hope for the fulfillment of large promises that are very much in the future. It *attaches* itself to the call and to the Caller and *detaches* itself from preferences that impede response to the call. It's as if the good changes color, shape, and the time of delivery because now there is a previously unimaginable good. Not seeing how that good can be obtained, Abraham has to believe and hope, not know and see. Obedience to the Someone who promised this good is another new ingredient introduced by the figure of Abraham. Abraham's good is epoch-making, differing from any understanding of the good that went before him.

The How of Right Desires

How to get from the right ideas about desires to right desires is not your everyday knowledge. I don't know anyone who has unlocked the process better than Ignatius. Fortunately, we don't have to guess about what Ignatius would say on how to get from being a nomad to living a life filled with holy desires. The dramatic process of their transformation as Ignatius himself experienced it is spelled out in detail for those conducting or making the *Spiritual Exercises*. In this section, I will note briefly several of Ignatius's insights into and suggestions for transforming desires as these are elaborated in the *Spiritual Exercises*.

The first reflection the retreatant is to make is uncanny in its significance for desire. I am to ponder the Christian truism that I was "created" and created with a purpose. The purpose God had in creating me was "to praise, reverence and serve God, our Lord, and by this means to save (my) soul."[3] But what is such a life if not a life of holiness? The main reason that desires multiply and collide or perplex and enslave is that one all-encompassing desire or end or purpose hasn't been internalized by the intender. When it is, one's desire pattern has a direction to go in, an end to seek. Rivulets can become a river going somewhere. Knowing that I was created for the praise and service of God can begin to bring vagrant desires into an alignment or expose the conflict with those out of kilter. Ignatius reminded the retreatant that, given this end, everything else is to be a means to attaining it, or one has to rid oneself of whatever is a hindrance to this end. Teleological clarity will confront one's past history of choosing goods for themselves or independently of the deeper purposes for which one was made. There will inevitably be tension because the good is beguilingly pluriform and the greater good isn't always evident. If there is no collision, then the greater good can begin to assume ascendency, and other desired goods will become relativized by it. If there is a collision of desires, the next set of considerations in the *Exercises* assists the person's being weaned from those that are disordered.

Ignatius the neophyte learned that God is most generous in the chamber of our desires when we ask them to be for what God wants. The *Exercises* recommend that we seek for the grace to abhor the disordered desires that have led to sin in the past or to being out of kilter with the end for which one was made. If one does not hate the personal history of sinful desires already yielded to, there will be little room for holy desires to emerge. Grace desired (which is already a grace) and implored, Ignatius was convinced, can bring about what unaided intellect and will cannot. At this point, the graces sought are for a repentance that will stir up a loathing for the sins that have caused the ways of God to become feeble in one's life. This whole process is a matter of degrees. The more the grace of repentance is sought for and received, the greater the loathing for sin will be, and the desire to live a life in union with the Holy One of God can grow commensurately. Christ is presented by Ignatius as the one whose crucifixion has freed me from the burden of my sins, a theme developed in the first chapter of this book. There is an opportunity to drink deeply of the truth that "for our sake he made him to be sin who did not know sin, so that we might become the [holiness] of God" (2 Cor. 5:21). Gratitude to him for his redeeming act can radically change a heart into one that loves and desires union with him.

Ignatius was sure that the church needed persons who could come around to conceiving and acting on great resolves born of great desires. He was equally sure that most could come to this degree of magnanimity if they sought and received the grace to deal with the little desires that distracted them from "great desires," which were desires to serve God and Jesus in their mission. It is impressive to see how well he himself accomplished his God-driven desire. Those who were formed by the *Exercises,* especially those who were directed by Ignatius himself, developed hearts passionate for the cause of Christ. They housed heaven's fire and came to burn with a love of Christ who personally became real to them. They grew free of their desires for disordered and disconnected goods so that they lived with a consuming zeal for what they usually called "souls." Francis Xavier is the best known of that initial company formed by Ignatius. Though the activities of the rest of them were not as worldwide nor as well known, they were no less intense and efficacious than Xavier's. This same formula of the *Exercises* is still effective. It has been estimated that more than one hundred thousand people have made the *Exercises* in some form this last year.

Having mastered his own aimlessness, he set out to "elicit great resolves and holy desires in others."[4] Convinced that having small resolves came from having little desires, he convinced others that their desires were sure to remain little if there were too many of them. The process Ignatius crafted trained hearts to go in one direction rather than in circles. Of themselves desires are not ordered. They have to be ordered. Going from small, multitudinous, all-over-the-place desires to great ones presumes a sensitivity to which are authentic and which are inauthentic. It also presumes a transcendent teleology. The smaller the desires, the more they proliferate. Many authentic desires generated in us by God are lost in scattered desires. Ignatius was scholastic enough to distrust any desire that did not somehow seem reasonable since desires alone were blind. They needed the eye of reason to see whether what they prompted was a true good or not. Even pious desires that were for the seemingly holy were not always to be followed as he discovered from his experience of following them and finding himself worse off for having been deluded by them.

One can study elsewhere Ignatius's wise rules for the discernment of the spirits operating in one's desires. Suffice it to say here that the main criterion of discernment for Ignatius was christological. He came to trust desires in himself that ran counter to his desire for his own honor. Consequently, he sought to cultivate desires in himself that honored Christ. This is why he trusted his own desire for poverty and humility. His experience was that the more one came to know and love Christ, the more one could develop "a nose" for what was redolent of his person. This is why the bulk of the *Spiritual Exercises* are meditations and contemplations and considerations on the person of Christ, knowing that it was actually possible to become sensitized to his person through guided prayer. Ignatius was sure that at the center of the transformation of desire was the Christ who could be known more intimately by the intellect and loved more ardently by the will and therefore followed more closely by the whole person. The story of Jesus could be gradually inhabited by means of the proposed meditations and contemplations. One's mind and, in turn, one's heart could begin to desire and enjoy union with him.

Ignatius's experience with desires was that they could be schooled and ordered by the disciplines of prayer focused on the person of Christ. But the *Exercises* introduce the retreatant to a distinctive Christ who is understood as having undertaken a worldwide campaign of winning women and men to serve the cause of assisting him in bringing about the reign of God. Many experience a distinct invitation to join him in this all-consuming enterprise. The bulk of the process of the *Spiritual Exercises* is spent introducing one to the person of Christ as if for the first time. The outcome sought is attachment to him with the aim of having oneself commit to a life of companionship with him. One can detach from pursuing aimless desires if one has something to be attached to. Detachment is in function of attachment to Christ and his cause and his companions.

For whatever it's worth, Ignatius would accept candidates to the Society of Jesus only if they so identified with Christ that they were willing to "suffer injuries, false accusations and affronts" because he had done so "for me."[5] If they couldn't say that this was so of them, they were to be asked whether they desired to desire these. If they couldn't say yes, they were not to be accepted in the Society. I raise this point only to underscore the centrality of desire and the centrality of Christ in the transformation of the affectivity needed for a total conversion. Affectivity is the necessary complement to ontology in this matter of holiness. By this I mean that God and the Son of God have done a marvelous thing in calling us to be holy people, but the response to this call has to be personally felt and acted on, in order for us to become who we already are.

In the first chapter I spoke of how marvelous the Christ-event is that has made us holy. It was done unto us. In this chapter it might seem I am contradicting myself, since it sounds like so much effort to become holy. Has holiness, in other words, ceased to be a receivement and reverted to being an achievement? No, the effort to be expended is in the direction of knowing what is already true of who you have been made by God. That has been done unto you so that "my joy might be in you and your joy might be complete" (John 15:11). There are so many contrary voices and so much fallacious material piled up over and obscuring the truth of our holiness that it takes an effort to unearth the treasure already buried in the field of our persons. That treasure is our "already holiness." Or, put in other terms, the holiness of God has been given to us to house. The bestowal of the fire was God's part. Our part is wanting to house it.

I believe that having a taste of the *Exercises* from the age of seventeen on is the reason that I found in myself the desire for a perfect companion already mentioned. I have experienced Christ to be that companion. I continue to experience in myself a need to be more faithful to and invested in this companionship. Having been conditioned Ignatianly, I also have the desire I mentioned earlier of wanting to be part of a cause that is vast and worthy of my life and commitment. What I have also discovered in the course of my continuing infidelities is that he does not intend this companionship to be an experience of the alone with the Alone. Companionship with Christ is a multimembered kind of experience.

There are several more things I want to say about this companionship. First of all, the experience is more in the area of augur and promise than something already fully possessed and enjoyed. Besides the continuing scatteredness of my desires as one reason for the companionship's not yet being wholly satisfying, there is also the fact that faith in this life does not deliver full sighting but sees through a glass darkly. But even more important, the more I get to know Christ, the more I experience him not as a solitary figure but as the many-membered person that Christian faith says he is. I increasingly experience him in and through the members of his body.

Perfectionism vs. Holiness

I feel the need at this point to distance this theme of holy desires from anything that smacks of a perfectionism with which it could be too closely associated. In Matthew 19:16–26 is a pericope about being free of a false, perfectionistic desire in order to follow a true one. In this passage, someone approaches Jesus with a question about the good he must do to possess eternal life. Jesus hears something slightly different that the man may not even have been conscious of, namely, that he was seeking perfection (Matt. 19:21), but at this point in the discourse Jesus says: "If you wish to enter into life, keep the commandments" (Matt. 19:17). That is not what the young man had in mind since he claimed he already knew and kept the commandments. Something greater than a moral rectitude was what he was seeking. The good he desired was more than moral good. Jesus then judged that for him this deeper good would be found only if his heart were free of the goods he had already amassed, apparently in great quantities (Matt. 19:22). As it turned out, he was not free to pursue his desire for a deeper good, apparently because of his accumulation over time of these lesser goods. The connection between his desire for something "more" and his freedom to go for it strikes a universal cord. While possessions are good, either they can weigh one down (as here), or dissatisfaction with them can lead one to a deeper desire (also here). In the same way, keeping the commandments makes one free, but that freedom is for more than a moral goodness. Hence, Jesus' invitation: "If you wish to be perfect, go, sell what you have and give to [the] poor, and you will have treasure in heaven. Then come, follow me" (Matt. 19:21). But the man's desire for a good he didn't know and now wouldn't know died in his heart. He turned away sad, snagged by lesser goods and unfree to find out in the walking what that deeper good was.

The measure of perfection for Matthew and early Christianity became companionship with the Christ. Insofar as one is in union with Christ, one is growing more perfect. Accepting his invitation to "come, follow me" (Matt. 19:21) should end forever other kinds of perfectionism that are striven for or performed into. Entrusting oneself to the relationship invited by Christ, the Holy One of God, is now the new measure of perfection. In addition to the infused virtues of faith, hope, and charity that are needed for entrusting oneself to him and the sevenfold gifts already mentioned in two previous chapters, entrusting oneself to this companionship brings with it an interior law, written on the heart. What is entailed now in being perfect is learned in the course of walking in truth and love in the Spirit with the Son, whose death and resurrection have enabled the companionship.

Measuring Perfection

Beginning with Plato there had always been a perceived need for having a measure—the Greeks called it a *metron*—an objective standard of judgment, about what constituted perfection or human flourishing that transcended the subjectivities with their many contradictory claims about what it was. For New Testament writers, companionship with Christ is now this measure of perfection or the foundational basis by which holiness is evaluated, gauged, judged. He becomes the principle before all principles, the norm that precedes all norms. He doesn't render principles or norms obsolete, just considerably less necessary. Moral normativity now yields pride of place to the existential measure of companionship, as in the episode just commented on. The good to be striven for now finds its measure in the fire of God's holiness, which has been embodied in Christ and with which one is imbued through faith in him. The true is now to be judged, with the assistance of the Spirit, by that "all wisdom" that will make each and every person "perfect" (Col. 1:28).

The previous measure of perfection used by Israel which was attunement to the law, had at times the unintended effect of making God unnecessary. It also at times developed a psychological heteronomy, meaning that the self is decentered by an *other,* a force or entity outside of itself, in this case the law. If it takes over the necessary autonomy of the self, it leaves persons alienated from themselves. Of course, autonomy alone is not going to flower into perfection either. Happily, there is a third possibility, namely, theonomy. Theonomy becomes one's spiritual and psychological condition when the love of God becomes the measure of the fullness one seeks. Only love can keep this measure from being a source of psychological heteronomy. Once I find that the promise of "fully assured understanding" can be found in the companion in whom dwells "all the treasures of wisdom and knowledge" (Col. 2:2–3), then theonomous is psychologically and religiously the most humanly perfect way to be. The *other* now is neither alien nor alienating to me, but my better self, my deeper self. The pearl of great price turns out to be the most enriching Friend I have.

Paul the Apostle expressed this experience in a number of ways. "For to me life is Christ" (Phil. 1:21) was one of these. "I live, no longer I, but Christ lives in me" (Gal. 2:20) was another. It is the Spirit that makes this degree of union, love, and self-entrustment

to the other conceivable, possible, and actual. The new law, ironi-
cally, is a companion. The only explanation for this is a pneuma-
tological one. The Spirit of Christ indwells, making Christ himself
the measure of our wisdom, sanctification, and redemption (1
Cor. 1:30). This measure is no longer exterior to us, commanding
oughts and ought nots, but in our hearts, generating wants for the
true and the good as he knows them and teaches us what they are.
The Gospel helps to keep this knowing measurable.

But so do "the least" (Matt. 25:31ff.). They are another way I
know this companion. I encounter him in the *koinōnia*, or community, of his suffering members (Phil. 3:10). Often they are more
a test of my faith than a reinforcement of companionship with
him. The losers, the lost, the last, the left behinds, the least seldom
sparkle with the degree of identification he has with them. While
Jesus assured us that whatever we do for and with these least, we
do it for him (Matt. 25:40), it often entails a huge act of faith
rather than an experience of companionship with him.

I have become aware that the measure of perfection is Christ
but in ways that are measured not only by the experience of a one-
to-one companionship with him. The measure of perfection for
all of us who adhere to him in faith is our gradually becoming
aware of him as a many who together "attain to the unity of faith
and knowledge of the Son of God, to mature manhood, to the
extent of the full statue of Christ" (Eph. 4:13). This is a remarkable
redefinition of perfection. It is no longer that of someone here and
someone there becoming perfect. The measure of perfection is an
"us" growing more one in knowledge of him whose perfection,
like ours, is future to us. But this perfection is also future to him
who is coming to full stature through us. There is a gradual
upbuilding of the body of Christ, "until we all attain to the unity
of faith and knowledge of the Son of God, to mature manhood, to
the extent of the full stature of Christ" (Eph. 4:13). This seems to

be an explosive bit of insight about perfection, not only that it is eschatological (that's remarkable enough) but also that it is developing by even now involving ourselves with one another to become that "mature manhood" (Jesus Christ) who is still coming to "full stature." This new information about perfection vaults the matter of being both one in faith with one another quite high and becoming one in the knowledge of God's Son equally high. In the context it is clear that Paul is sure this growth in knowledge of him comes about horizontally (by our growth in solidarity) as well as vertically (by our union or copresence with God). The letter of Ephesians goes on with the exhortation "living the truth in love, we should grow in every way into him who is the head, Christ, from whom the whole body, joined and held together by every supporting ligament, with the proper functioning of each part, brings about the body's growth and builds itself up in love" (Eph. 4:15–16). Fullness lies before us, but even the present Christ's fullness lies before him. Growth in him is that of a collectivity being formed into that perfect man, the Christ, who has still to come to "full stature."

The more I experience this companion through the latticework of his members, the more it appears that whatever holiness grows in us is both an already thing and also a not-yet thing. The not-yet holy grows into the already insofar as we walk in love with the wonderful-to-be-with as well as with the woe-betides who are less wonderful to be with. I find the metaphor of walking in the Spirit a rich one in this regard. One doesn't choose to be holy! One is called to be by God. Nor does one choose all the ways in which this holiness grows. One discovers in the walking how to grow in God's holiness. Suffice it to say that this many-membered companion is unlike any other we could possibly have or imagine in this world. It takes our best to adore him when he shows up in "the least." Perfectionism in any of its forms will weigh anyone down who confuses the call to holiness with being without imperfection. God's strategy for Christian holiness is not perfection but friendship with his Son in all his guises. "Who now do you say that I am?" I say you are a many splendored and a many bedraggled Person through whom the whole bunch of us grows "joined and held together by every supporting ligament" into you as the whole "builds itself up in love" (Eph. 4:16).

Angelism

As long as I have perfectionism on the run, let me add angelism. Recall that the Second Vatican Council sees a holy life as "a more human way of life." It is necessary to distance our very human desires from any conception of holiness that smacks of angelism. Angelism denies my deep oneness with the cheetah, the rabbit, even the grass. If holiness is construed as some kind of transcendence from materiality, sexuality, or physicality it will be false. I don't leave earth by walking into the holiness of God. I am grounded by my materiality and physicality and by the limitations that flesh is heir to. In putting on Christ, we take on, and fully accept, our own humanity as if for a second time as he did for the first time with the incarnation. Putting on Christ entails accepting our humanity in all its mortality, corruptibility, finitude, and entropy. It is in the midst of, not in spite of, these constraints that we are saved and made whole. A disembodied holiness is a head trip, a metaphysical gargoyle, a category mistake. It is not only through my being consubstantial with material reality that I become holy, but even through the reality of sin, my own and others'. War, divorce, addiction, poverty, suffering, crime, floods, and so on are the unpromising materials with which the Weaver weaves the sanctity by which God is praised and with which God is pleased.

Angelism has been particularly successful in getting us to be ashamed of our sexuality and the desires that emerge from it. Sexuality is meant to be sacramental—not denied, therefore, but lifted or sublated to friendship with God and our human companions. An asexual relationality could hardly issue in the self-emptying love of one another that Christ had in mind when he left us the one commandment. Obeying the commandment to love one another usually includes sexual abstinence, presumably motivated by the good of the other, the common good, and the prior fidelities one has committed to. Probably the closest we can come to knowing how God loves us is by the human experience of being in love because one then learns to care about every aspect of the life of the loved one. Without this human experience it is likely that the totality of God's love of us would remain more an object of belief than the experience it ideally should be. But being in love inevitably requires dealing with one's sexuality. When angelism takes the form of a denial of one's sexuality, it will make one indifferent to love and, therefore, to human holiness. And to confine one's understanding of sexuality merely to the morality or immorality of sexual acts misses the vocational and relational dimensions of holiness. In saying this I do not presume that human flourishing and a healthy relational life necessitate genital sexual activity. But by the same token all our expressions of love of one another are in some way sexual because we are necessarily sexual beings. Angelism can't praise God because it denies something precious about what God has made.

A final introspective look into my desire pattern surfaces two certainties: (1) sexual desire is part of that pattern, and (2) it is not my deepest desire. This perfect-mate desire is the deeper desire, namely, for someone who understands me even better than I understand myself and accepts me even better than I accept myself and whom I feel safe entrusting myself to. Yet, again trying to plumb my desires, this relationship wouldn't leave me where I am but would bring out the best in me, better than I could ever do alone. This friend wouldn't want anything in return from me except the time and attention it takes for our relationship to grow in mutuality and love. Since you become what you love, we would begin to think the same way, have the same concerns and interests. Our loves and our loathings become more and more the same. The cost for entering into that degree of communion is the surrender of the individualism that wants to "do it my way." The gain is in a mutuality of purpose and a communion of mind and heart. I find that in knowing Christ, I begin to meet these desires.

Longing

I began this chapter with the intention of keeping holiness real, so I will end it with what I think is probably true of most of us who are doing our best to be Christian. I suspect for most of us our experience of God and Christ is not of the holiness with which God has actually imbued us but of longing for the Holy One. But this longing is just as surely the work of God as holiness is. Holiness invariably brings longing with it. "My soul longs for you, O God./My being thirsts for God, the living God" (Ps. 42:2–3). This graced longing creates an empty space that has God at the center of it. The longing for God cannot be explained except by a love for one who is already known.

Psychologically, one couldn't long for someone who is wholly unknown. The longing is for the living God, who has already made a home in us. God is not so absent that there is only emptiness. An emptiness that doesn't know what the emptiness is for would be a dangerous condition to be in since there would be the felt need to assuage it with some immediate "good." Graced longing includes an awareness of what is longed for. Without that knowledge the longing would be dispiriting and a source of unpeace and unhappiness. With that knowledge, however, the longing is positive and cleansing. "Blessed are they who hunger and thirst for [holiness]/for they will be satisfied" (Matt. 5:6). Focused longing is from God. Indecipherable emptiness is not.

We long for a good that is absolutely good, good without limit, wholly good, therefore wholly lovable. What is this but the good that is God? The holy is the good off the chart, an unlimited, time-transcending, complete, perfect good. The holy is God. The holy is not an object. It is a condition and a horizon. The kingdom of God on the lips of Jesus functioned as such a notion in his life. He longed for its completion and knew its inception. "The kingdom of heaven is like a merchant searching for fine pearls. When he finds a pearl of great price, he goes and sells all that he has and buys it" (Matt. 13:45–46). Holiness is a good of such transcendent stature and value that all the other pearls shrink by comparison and will be forfeited, if necessary, to possess such a treasure.

The church uses the season of Advent to teach Jesus' followers the disciplines of the heart that learn to wait for the Lord who is also Immanuel, God with us, but who is not always experienced as being with us. The Advent prayer is *Marana, tha,* "Lord, come!" Or, a variation on this is even more a prayer of hope, *Maran atha,* "The Lord is coming." Those who learn the discipline of knowing what they are hoping for and of waiting for it "will renew their strength,/they will soar as with eagles' wings;/They will run and not grow weary,/walk and not grow faint" (Isa. 40:31).

The deer fortunately knows that it thirsts for running streams. The same Greek verb, *dipsaō,* can be translated as either "long for" or "thirst." On the last and greatest day of the festival Jesus stood up and cried out: "Let anyone who thirsts come to me and drink." (John 7:37). If this drink will come from him, how will it come? "Rivers of living water will flow from within [the one who is thirsting]" (John 7:38). How will these rivers of living water come about? Jesus was referring to "the Spirit that those who came to believe in him were to receive. There was, of course, no Spirit yet, because Jesus had not yet been glorified" (John 7:39). So, blame the Spirit of holiness for our thirst. We can also thank the Spirit of holiness for the slaking of the thirst that is for the living God. If we don't know that this is what we are thirsting for, the Spirit would be happy to teach us. So, "knock and [it] will be opened to you" (Matt. 7:7).

5

Holy Stretching and the Glory of God

HOLINESS IS A GIFT already given and a challenge that is never withdrawn. But responding to this challenge is easily misconstrued. There is enough residual Pelagianism in each of us to think that though holiness is given by God, we're on our own if there is to be any growth in holiness. I believe this idea of our growing in holiness is not a particularly useful image. Preferable is the Pauline metaphor of walking, because it better illustrates the role the Spirit plays in our relation to God's holiness in us. We are already holy because of Christ, but we walk in holiness because of the Spirit. Anthropologically, we walk from less complete to more complete. We are built to walk because of an eros propelling us ever forward. This eros is to know and to love and to be known and loved. Because of this urge for a fullness we can taste but haven't attained, we just can't stand still. While eros in its two primary forms prompts our walking, how we walk and for what are another matter. This chapter will examine this "how" and "for what" in the light of the holiness we are called to.

But first, I must say something about eros. In early Greek mythology, Eros was a child born of need and resourcefulness. My eros and yours are born of these same two parents. Intrinsic to the human condition is the need to know and to love and to have these reciprocated. Our resourcefulness drives us in the direction of self-transcendence. It is always a drive for more that has to be obeyed. To disregard it or to try a total quenching of it would be deeply disobedient to the way we have been scripted by our Creator. But eros is also capable of great folly if its drive is mindless. The Greeks saw eros needing to be cultivated by two constant influences: *paideia* (the refinement of education) and *sophia* (wisdom). We will seek some of this refinement and wisdom in this chapter. While we have enormous energy for self-transcendence propelled by the eros with which we have been scripted, it is by no means automatic that we will walk in the direction of our flourishing.

Paul, as usual, concretely describes how this happens for those who are in Christ. To walk in and into holiness is to walk in the Spirit. And he has a particularly helpful image about how this kind of walking happens that differentiates it from other walking. It is a walking that stretches the walker, that forces walkers to expand their gait so that the distance to the end point sought for is shortened not by each physical stride but by a movement that has an integrity to it. Paul describes himself as constantly "straining forward to what lies ahead" since "I for my part do not consider myself to have taken possession" (Phil. 3:13). The Greek term he uses is from the verb *epekteinein,* meaning to stretch or expand or push on or run toward. In just this one verb we can appreciate the single-mindedness of Paul. "I continue my pursuit [as *I run*] *toward* the goal, the prize of God's upward calling, in Christ Jesus" (Phil. 3:14). He runs toward it, stretches toward it, and with each step shortens the distance between himself and the finish line.

This image of stretching is helpful for understanding how our holiness is in play in the human everyday order of things. There are, of course, always two agencies at work in this process, the human and the divine. Pelagians were only half right, therefore. Our human effort contributes this natural, ever-striving, never-satisfied eros. I am a natural stretcher. I am not satisfied with what I know or with the love I receive and give. Hence, my ever stretching forward. Then there is the divine agency in the person of the Spirit, which usually enters the human realm so quietly and reverently that it is virtually imperceptible. Would that the Spirit's entries into our consciousness were ecstatic, leaving us with no response except an awed yes! But the Spirit's movement is seldom, if ever, so blatant. So the human agent must recognize the meek entry of the divine and how it would suffuse the human. Ignatius likened the process to a drop of water entering a sponge. Without the recognition of each entry stretching one toward a greater good, one is caught up in a cycle of satisfying an ignorant eros without "attention on the finish line." One is stretching then, but not in one direction.

This notion of *epektasis* (stretching) in Paul would probably have been overlooked had it not been for the attention brought to it by Gregory of Nyssa (ca. 335–ca. 394). He ruminated on how "the actual good, even if it appears the greatest and the most perfect possible, is never anything but the beginning of a superior good. Consequently, here also is verified the word of the apostle Paul that, by *epectasy* toward what is ahead, the things which had formerly appeared fall into oblivion."[1] Gregory was tasting the paradox of his own heart when he commented that "the one limit of perfection is the fact that it has no limit" (Ibid.). I would go a step further by suggesting that God too is stretching toward us, that God too is divine Eros. With the help of the Spirit we are "of one mind and heart" with God.

Perhaps a good analogue of this stretching process is the consequence to Mary of the entry into her womb of the Spirit of God. Her womanhood was not violated by the event of her pregnancy. She had nothing to do with having been called, but she had much to accept in having been called for this awesome role. There is some hint here about how the Spirit, which came upon her and overshadowed her, functions in the human order. As with her, so also with ourselves, we must be aware of and accept having been chosen to be made holy by God. But we must also choose in an ongoing way the challenge of our holiness. The rules are akin to those of a mother carrying an embryo, a fetus, an infant. It grows on its own, yet at the same time, it depends on the vigilance of the carrier to protect it from any harmful influence. Mary's awareness was key to the fetus's well-being and carrying it to term. There were no days off. The same holds true for us.

Since holiness takes more and more room, a parallel growth in emptiness is one of the conditions of its increase. *Godly* describes only in part who you are at present. It must also stand for who you are allowing yourself to become. God's holiness isn't housed comfortably where there is already a full plate or satiation or where there is something else winning all the affection or absorbing the attention of the carrier. Holiness neither ignores nor circumvents nor disdains nor violates the nature in which it grows. It perfects it. Necessarily, this involves some discipline of natural eros on the part of the carrier, since the two are not one— nature is not yet wholly graced, two wills are not synchronous. The analogy with a fetus is not perfect, of course (no analogy is; otherwise, it's not an analogy), since the carrier in Mary's case is also carried by the one she is carrying. It is also imperfect since the two eventually separate. It is imperfect, furthermore, since Mary presumably does not cease to stretch after the birth. With our own holiness there isn't separation, since one's whole humanity is brought into and participates in the life of the Trinity until "God becomes all in all." Finally, as with Mary, so also with us, there is a kind of death to the carrier since she who "wished to save [her] life will lose it." But it is only a kind of a death since she who "loses [her] life . . . will save it" (Mark 8:35).

Holiness is a stretch. We are stretched, and we accept being stretched, but it is not a stretch that we initiate. Although the stretch begins with the eros of our never-satisfied, restless human nature, the step is initiated by the help of God's Eros toward us. God's Eros is the Spirit sent by the Father and the Son. It is the Spirit that enables our stretching toward God. "The love of God has been poured out into our hearts through the holy Spirit that has been given to us" (Rom. 5:5). The stretch in the direction of God will not attract us unless we have received the love of the One stretching us and proceed in the direction we are moved to walk into. We can love both the direction and the One stretching us only because God has first loved us and poured forth into our hearts this gift of Love that is the Holy Spirit. What we walk away from when we walk in the Spirit is the old self, the false self, the flesh that is passing away, the eros that is blind and self-centered. What we walk in and into is the holiness of God.

How does this happen, more specifically? As I have already indicated, it seems it is directly connected to the eros character of our human nature. The Spirit penetrates our natural eros which is both to know reality, what is real and true, and to love the good. According to tradition, the usual way this process takes place in the intellect and the will of the person is by the gifts of the Holy Spirit. Each of these gifts stretches us with understanding, wisdom, counsel, and knowledge. These gifts kick in and abet the human eros to know. In the same way, the human will to love is strengthened by the gifts of fear of the Lord, courage, and piety. Activation of one of these sevenfold gifts is the tradition's way of

explaining how the Spirit stretches those who, already in the
Spirit, respond to the call to holiness.

Stretching and the Glory of God

A walk is successful only if one has a purpose and a destination.
What is the destination the Spirit prompts? That's the easier
question. Union with God seems like the obvious answer. The
more difficult issue is whether the Spirit prompts in us the purpose of growing in holiness. I don't believe this is the case. That
seems too self-centered. Or it could induce a perfectionism or a
scrupulosity. Besides, there is always a degree of indecipherability
in this matter of holiness that could invite self-deception. But
even more to the point: we don't grow in holiness by intending to.
One of the parables is enlightening about this. "This is how it is
with the kingdom of God; it is as if a man were to scatter seed on
the land and would sleep and rise night and day and the seed
would sprout and grow, he knows not how. Of its own accord the
land yields fruit, first the blade, the the ear, then the full grain in
the ear" (Mark 4:26–28).

It seems much closer to the mark to say that the Spirit
prompts in us not the purpose of growing in holiness but the purpose of glorifying God. The eros to know and to love is always
prompting a desire for more, and the indwelling Spirit is ever
about the process of clarifying in us what this more is that we
crave. To what end are these two huge eros turbines, our hearts
and minds, moving us? I believe the Spirit takes the dynamism
these two engines generate and moves them in the direction of
God and God's glory. I believe the best expression of what the
Spirit prompts in us by way of purpose in this matter of holiness

is encapsulated by Paul: "Whether you eat or drink, or whatever you do, do [all] for the glory of God" (1 Cor. 10:31).

To do all for the glory of God decenters our concern about our holiness. What would be entailed if one were to live so as to do all for the glory of God? Negatively: not being so self-regarding that my own "glory" or honor would hinder my desire to choose what is for God's glory. Positively: being sufficiently God-regarding that my consciousness has a sense of the reality of God in the thoughts, words, and deeds that continually express my reality. This awareness of God admits of many degrees, of course, from the subliminal to many explicit forms. This awareness can be prompted by awe or love or desire for or fear of God. It could take the form of explicit prayer in its many expressions or a simple advertence. As it becomes more explicit, this awareness can be more in the form of praise and worship than of petition, though this latter is never without merit as the Our Father's many petitions indicate. Since God has already glorified us by enabling us to be participants in the life of the Trinity itself, our responses to having been elevated to this stature must reflect this and give glory to God. The Our Father is a window into Jesus "stretching." "Our Father, hallowed be thy name, thy kingdom come, thy will be done on earth as it is in heaven."

"Whether you eat or drink, or whatever you do, do [all] for the glory of God" (1 Cor. 10:31). There is much wisdom in Paul's mandate to do all for the glory of God. Having received God's holiness, or heaven's fire, if you will, we respond to it by doing all for the glory of God. This takes the focus off the self and posits it on the source of the self's creation, justification, reconciliation, and holiness. But Paul is saying more than this. He is saying that he undertakes and undergoes all the pedestrian things in his life, doing them and suffering them, with the express purpose of glorifying God. I need to examine this process more concretely now.

Eros and Knowing

I am a news junkie. Part of every day is spent finding out what's going on in the world—the world of politics, the world of sports, the world of international events, the world of religion, the worlds of weather and personalities and public figures, and so on. I feel incomplete if I go to bed at night not having heard or read or seen the news. Here I want to look at this part of my everyday routine in light of the preceding section. I had always viewed this part of my daily doings as religiously neutral. But another look at it has begun to make me think differently. (While I will examine one part of my daily routine in these terms, you, the reader may have some other area that occupies or preoccupies you. In that case, you will be able to see my reflection as commenting on your equivalent of being a news junkie.)

Every time I turn on the television or the radio or pick up the paper, I am inviting something into my consciousness. My consciousness is both my inner sanctum and that part of me that is in touch with everything beyond me. In evolutionary terms, it was around fifteen billion years before anything living on earth began to display this quality of consciousness. In moral terms, my consciousness, what I let into it and what I dismiss, neglect, or block are my responsibility. In epistemological terms, consciousness is my door to self-transcendence. Of course, I can self-transcend into the soup of the ignoble or inane or untrue. By the same token and via the same route, I can gain access to the real, the true, the good.

"Whether you eat or drink, or whatever you do, do [all] for the glory of God" (1 Cor. 10:31). Is it neurotic to believe that the appropriate response to the holiness I have received, as Paul was exhorting the Corinthians to do in this text, entails taking each thing I do, such as eating or drinking or reading the paper, into some kind of alignment with glorifying God? I don't believe so. The context of this Corinthian quotation about doing *all* for the glory of God is Paul's feeling a great expansiveness of spirit because of the freedom he came to experience in Christ. Hence, now "everything is lawful" for him, like eating foods sacrificed to idols because "the earth and all its fullness are the Lord's" (1 Cor. 10:23, 26). Isn't it only right, therefore, that the *all* that belongs to the Lord should be referred back to its Source? This is easy enough to see about the more significant moments of the day when all systems are firing, so that moments of work, prayer, ministry, or relationship should be done for the glory of God. But since there is something total about being in the new creation—*all,* not just *some,* of what one does should be of a piece with responding to this reality of glorifying God.

So, I must ask myself what it is I am seeking when I'm inquiring to know anything, like hearing the news. Does simply getting information explain this ever-present itch? If so, what is so important about being informed? Being uninformed is surely nothing to aim at, of course, but what am I intending by being informed? It seems that it is endemic to the eros of my own spirit, and as far as I can tell, to everyone else's, to want to know more about what is real, about what is going on in our world—if for no other reason than that being in the dark can get one blindsided. Undertaking a news search is an act of self-transcendence, an effort to move out of ignorance into knowledge about "what's up."

What does acquiring this kind of information have to do with glorifying God? Nothing, unless I make it have something to do with it. There is the issue of the use of the talent of consciousness and my guardianship and use of it. Notice the several distinct operations that go on when one reads the paper, watches the news on television, or catches it on the radio. First of all, I am experiencing what is new or of interest. Second, I can also enjoy some degree of understanding of what I am being informed about. I am even aware, third, of sometimes making a judgment about what I have read or heard, assenting or withholding assent, or pigeon-holing it in some mental file until I learn more about it. Finally, I can intend some action or change of attitude or make some decision about what I am going to do, if anything, about the acquired information.

There's another dimension of consciousness beyond the fact that it is triggered by objects gaining my attention. Consciousness cannot be experienced without the "out there" object evoking some feeling. Consciousness is seldom activated without developing some feeling about the object being attended to. It is this feeling evoked by the object that raises the mind and heart to the intended object that, in turn, has the potential for raising the mind and the heart to God. Our intentionality can mature into glorifying God or function in a lesser way by remaining at an immanent level, where the object attended to stays at the object attended to, period.

As we saw in the third chapter, there is in a consciousness of an object a horizon within which the object is beheld. It helps to be conscious of one's consciousness and its horizon in developing any intentionality. First of all, it helps to become more conscious of the difference between the times our consciousness is acting with an awareness of the horizon of faith and when it is not. Faith sees things in a new light. There is clearly a difference between seeing beyond what we see immediately and acting with love in contrast to when we are not so seeing or acting. Sometimes the difference is more evident than at other times.

To be more specific, I can read the paper in two ways and with two different mind-sets. One is from within a horizon that is actively God-aware. This will affect my feelings at times about what is being ingested. These feelings can run the gamut: compassion or revulsion or hope or identification with or joy or concern or fear or anger or complicity or boredom or simple fascination, and so on. These feelings can lead to a form of subliminal prayer or to explicit sentiments of praise or thanks, petition or reparation, depending on what my consciousness is attending to on a given page. Or I can read the paper by simply taking the data it supplies into my various mental operations that raise my mind and heart to the object but without seeing beyond the object itself. This is a consciousness that is horizon-vacant. My consciousness apprehends the object as autonomous and leaves it in its autonomy. In the first of these two ways, the reading of the newspaper has forged the bonds in my heart with God, howsoever briefly or slightly. In the second way it hasn't. It has, therefore, extended my appropriation of some aspect of the world without having that appropriation affect my God horizon. This is not a moral failure, of course. There is much about the news that warrants our approaching it pragmatically. But as an exercise in religious neutrality, it is an opportunity lost as far as holiness is concerned. Paul would say, I think, that I have done something that falls short of glorifying God. God was parked on the side while I got on with being informed.

I have become impressed by some of Bonaventure's insights in this connection. Being of a contemplative bent of mind, and with considerably less information at his fingertips than we moderns have, Bonaventure was in the habit of asking himself what it is that he was searching for at the outset of each of his inquiries. Each of the things he came to understand, therefore, he would see as a ladder that enabled him to behold them within the overarching truth and presence of God; each discrete reality was somehow glimpsed in light of its origin and destiny. So any new information could become not just self-transcending but an occasion for touching even the Transcendent. I'm not sure what he would do with the news as we know it today, but my suspicion is that it would be taken into the horizon of his vision of reality in which all things are seen in the light of their "origin, greatness, plenitude, activity and order" in God.[2]

Bonaventure inveighed against a fragmented pursuit of knowledge. For him its acquisition ideally was always in alignment with one end, namely, union with its Source. So the intellectual, moral, and contemplative directions of his life became parts of a whole. Taking a cue from him, I can ask about the purpose of the information I am always seeking. To what end am I seeking it? To what extent is its pursuit, however momentary and important or innocuous, done within a horizon or with a consciousness of one's deeper eros and purpose? Presumably it is seldom so viewed, and the only end I am conscious of is very immediate, that is, finding out what there is to know that I won't know unless I read the paper or view the television or listen to the radio or scan the Internet. Such a short-sighted telos, or end, might be worthy of my humanity, but is it worthy of the holiness I have received?

I can read the paper for its own sake and for whatever I derive from its perusal. It is what it is, period. Or I can read the paper like a Bonaventure, therefore, with a much more active horizon and faith consciousness. Like Paul, Bonaventure strove to do all for the glory of God, even the seemingly innocuous. Anything he did, therefore, was open to and affected by his contemplative attitude. This wasn't trying to do two things at once, but it was simply expecting "to find God in all things," as Ignatius Loyola would later put it. For both of these giants, love united and forged unities between what otherwise would have been kept separate. Both of them prompt the question: Ought our end to be so all-encompassing that we do all for the glory of God? Paul, I believe, would not hesitate to say yes. When we separate our sense of purpose from the primary reason of our being—the glorification of God—the area of the religiously neutral grows, while consciousness of our holiness becomes sporadic and ineffectual.

The presumption in advocating such a central place for the glory of God is that one's consciousness has already been and continues to be shaped by faith. If this is not the case, encounters with news, information, data, and so on will surely remain simply what they are. But if it has, and continues to be, then such moments more easily travel on to be shaped by faith. The shaping of one's faith horizon takes place best in the act of praying. But such an alignment cannot be taken for granted simply because one has been "raised religiously" or is a person of faith. God must be real enough to the person to have his or her ultimate horizon continually reinforced. Consciousness alone is prone to vagrancy, noncommitment, even amnesia. Without an ongoing ideological reinforcement, some degree of constancy in one's prayer life is necessary.

Inspired by Bonaventure and Ignatius, I return to this question of what the end is of the particular information I am seeking. What end do I have in mind in my inquiry? Information and knowledge, of course. Accurate knowledge! True information! Knowledge of the truth of the reality in which I live and which I seek to understand and judge. The eros of the human spirit is for knowledge of the truth. I was scripted to know as much about reality as I can take in, which is why I am endlessly wanting to know as much as I can. It seems provable that human consciousness is the apex of God's creation. We already glorify God simply by employing it. A consciousness that is not merely functioning well but is functioning with an ongoing awareness of its Source— this is the consummation devoutly to be wished. Surely this is what glorifies God. God's holiness was given to us to grow in acknowledging the Source from which these two marvels, consciousness and holiness, come. Appreciating these two divine accomplishments, together or separately, glorifies God.

Besides the obvious spiritual value of going in this direction, it is also psychologically healing. This, of course, presumes that we know what the illness is. We could call it the syndrome of channel surfing. A more sophisticated term would be multiphrenia. A multiphrenic works within a multiplicity of disconnected or conflicting frames of reference, which leaves his or her conciousness fragmented. Modern technology has rather rapidly increased the possibility of this multiphrenia. So ubiquitous are these different lenses that the multiphrenia that would have been considered a pathology at one time seems now to be enjoying an air of normalcy. Just as a fast-darting consciousness in another is hard to relate to, so too the same darting consciousness in oneself makes it hard to settle down, or even to know who you are. All of which is to say that a consciousness that holds steady to the reality and challenge of holiness—which should have one do all for the glory due to God—will be increasingly difficult to maintain if, as a contemporary "viewer," I do not take greater control over my use of the vast range of "channels" available to me. Consciousness is too precious to waste.

Multiphrenia is healed insofar as one's teleology is in place. What channel surfers seek by surfing all over the place can be found if they are clearer about what they are seeking. We are able to be happy magi if we "see his star in the east" and follow it. We are certain to be unhappy, meandering magi if we follow every star, seeing one as no brighter or more alluring than another, and never "close the deal." Growing in an awareness of what/who is stretching us toward our end through the everyday world of the objects that endlessly migrate into our consciousness—this glorifies God.

Each existent in the infrahuman world of created reality has no problem "knowing" its teleology. It is written into each pebble and mountain and sea and deer and rose. Each of these has no problem because it is scripted to do and become what it does and becomes. And since this is so, each thing acting from its particular script glorifies God. Just by being and doing as its "laws" determine it, God is being glorified. This line of reflection produces in me the uncomfortable thought that maybe all these creatures, singly and collectively, now and for thousands of previous years, have been glorifying God so much better than I or most of us humans do. Our human way of glorifying God has to come through our consciousness with its drives to know and to love. But these do not automatically move to right knowing and right loving. Once we get the hang of these, there's no end to the glory we can give to God in comparison to the rest of creation.

What is the teleology or finality of this natural eros to know? It seems obvious that information is for knowledge. And knowledge is information analyzed. Knowledge is more than opinion, which is unverified knowledge. We want our knowledge to be accurate or at least probable and as trustworthy as possible. The true, the truth, is the summit and telos of knowledge. Truth is valuable and usable. Some of it is valuable for judging rightly. Some of it is valuable for living rightly. The telos of truth is wisdom. Truth comes to rest in wisdom. Wisdom is the cumulative effect of knowing the truth and living in obedience to it. Actions are wise when taken from wisdom. Ideally wisdom takes the measure of our actions before and after the fact.

Plato's contribution to understanding wisdom was to see it as the quality of putting things in order. The wise person puts order where otherwise there isn't order. Aristotle's contribution to understanding wisdom was to see it coming about as a result of contemplation, which for him was the highest action anyone could undertake. For him contemplation was done for its own sake, not with any practical purpose in mind. Augustine's understanding of wisdom was to see the role love played in seeking to come to wisdom. Wisdom was a taste that could be developed because of the love of what was contemplated. Wisdom in Latin *(sapientia)* is from the verb *sapere*, "to taste or savor." Some things can be known only if they are savored with the heart. In the heart, knowing can become wisdom. Action done from wisdom glorifies God.

This is all nonsense, of course, to those raised in the information age who have come to think that information is the zenith of our consciousness. For them, information is enough; it has no other end. What is being forgotten in the information age is the insight of these ancients that wisdom is behind our quest for knowledge or our eros for knowing. When complemented by the Christian faith, our eros knows its telos, the end that propels our desire to know, the vision of total Truth, which is God.

The beginning of T. S. Eliot's "Choruses from 'The Rock'" says it well:

> All our knowledge brings us nearer to our ignorance,
> All our ignorance brings us nearer to death,
> But nearness to death no nearer to God.
> Where is the life we have lost in living?
> Where is the wisdom we have lost in knowledge?
> Where is the knowledge we have lost in information?
> The cycles of Heaven in twenty centuries
> Bring us farther from God and nearer to the Dust!

Here I have tried to harness our omnipresent consciousness to see how it might serve the glory of God through the everyday pedestrian operations of the human mind. When consciousness is glorifying God, it is fulfilling the end for which it was made. I have examined only one pedestrian use of the eros to know: everyday news. There are any number of others. There are sports junkies, bridge junkies, crossword-puzzle junkies, political junkies, car junkies, and so forth. But there are more refined interests such as Shakespeare, the opera, astrophysics, and so on. Regardless of the interest, one must be careful not to allow one's consciousness to become preoccupied by these pursuits. Since we are not compelled to glorify God through these interests but rather allow them to distract us from this purpose, it is time to evaluate things anew.

Eros and Loving

There is a second area of our lives that can and should glorify God, namely, our relationships with one another. Not only in our ordinary and extraordinary knowing but also in our ordinary and extraordinary loving, God can be glorified. The sanctifying Spirit moves the natural eros for knowing and for loving into a drive for more. For more what? Bernard Lonergan sees the Spirit as enabling one to be in love "without limits or qualifications or conditions or reservations. Just as unrestricted questioning is our capacity for self-transcendence, so being in love in an unrestricted fashion is the proper fulfillment of that capacity."[3] If one were to love God without reservation, one would be housing heaven's fire. But this is why the fire of love was given. "The love of God has been poured out into our hearts through the holy Spirit that has been given to us" (Rom. 5:5).

Let me begin by distinguishing between two very different kinds of relationships. Erotic relationships are those that seek merely to satisfy the self. They do not transcend the self but seek merely its own gratification. These don't need to be commented on since I presume that it doesn't take much reflection for them to show themselves for what they are. God obviously will not be glorified by relationships that never transcend the erotic. But there is a whole series of eros loves that most people enjoy, that is, with friends, family, spouse, children, that evoke varying degrees of self-transcendence and varying degrees of love. Like their mythic parent, Eros, these loves are born of need and resourcefulness. Presumably one's most valued relationships are those of marriage and family, but eros loving does not stop there. It can also generate relations of altruism, solidarity, loyalty, and community. Eros obeyed generates energy and creativity. Eros disobeyed makes for mopey, dispirited, unfulfilled humans.

The particular point I want to reflect on here is how these eros-driven loves are or might be connected to the *agapē*-love that is characteristic of God. *Agapē*-love is love poured out. It is pure giving. *Agapē*-love has its origin in the Trinity and reveals how God is triune. *Agapē*-love generates the relations of pure giving that has God "beget" God as Son and in turn, has Love proceed from this totality of mutuality as a distinct "Person." This agapic self-donation has also become "flesh" in the incarnate holiness of Jesus of Nazareth and after that in varying degrees in all those who have received this *agapē*-gift, which is the Spirit who enables the receiver literally to participate in the ambit of these pure, self-giving divine relations.

We will inquire into our relationships with one another vis-à-vis *agapē*-love. There are three possible attitudes one can have about his or her eros loves. The first of these is the disconnected kind of relationship. This is the same as the attitude commented on about the news in the first half of the chapter. Just as the news is the news is the news—it is what it is—so also my eros-loves are what they are. My relationship with God and these human relationships are apples and oranges. They don't connect. I have my friends, and I have my faith, and they connect only if there is loss, for example, by death, or by conflict, because a moral challenge develops in the relationship. Otherwise, they remain each in its own order and remain disconnected.

I don't agree with this attitude. It is not a theologically accurate understanding of the self any more than it is of eros relationships or God or holiness. Unfortunately, there is considerable theological opinion favoring this disconnection thesis. I think of the classic work of Anders Nygren, *Eros and Agapē*, which left these two different kinds of relationship too disconnected. For Nygren, *agapē*-love, which is God's love, is meant only to confront our eros-loves; otherwise they are not connected.[4] But disconnecting these two has the effect of secularizing our human experiences of love. It ensures that we will live in a condition of dualism if we try to be people of faith while also cultivating relationships of eros-love, because these latter will then have a life of their own since the faith life has taken on such an otherworldly character. This attitude makes it easy to think that eros relationships are of no religious value, presumably even consigning them to a part of this world that is passing away.

This first position is theologically wrongheaded because the drive of eros to self-transcendence through love is not only good and essential to human flourishing, but, being love, it must already be of God at least to some degree. If human nature were evil, then eros loves would be tarred by the same brush. Since human nature and this drive that is internal to it aren't evil, a different theological evaluation of eros-love has to be developed.

A second position holds that, speaking generally and abstractly, people usually have sufficient insight about which relationships are good (eros driven) and which aren't (erotic). This second position posits a harmony between the cultivation of human eros-loves and God's *agapē*-love. It reasons that where love is, God is. All love is from God. Love is indivisible, whether it begins from below in human relationships or from above.

This second theological position intuits and seeks to further develop a greater harmony between one's faith life and one's eros life. It is optimistic about the self and its "nature" as it is wired to meet its needs, seeing the Author of nature behind the wiring.

This theological optimism makes it easier to find God in one's relationships. Friends can even be seen as embodied graces with which God has gifted us. Hence, this position sees, at the very minimum, a continuum between human and divine love, whereas the first position sees only a discontinuity.

This second position is theologically more credible than the first one. But the problem with this second one is its likely naïveté about eros-loves. Since these usually develop a mind of their own, discernment of their quality is not helped by positing a harmony between eros-loves and *agapē*-love prematurely. I say prematurely not because I think there can't be a continuum between these two kinds of love but because it can't be presumed before the fact or as necessarily continuing to be true in the course of the relationship. It must be worked at. It isn't automatic or intrinsic to eros-love that it is one with *agapē*-love. The primary limitation in eros-love is that insofar as the relationship is meeting one's personal needs, it is unlikely that what is born of eros is wholly without some self-seeking. Granted, eros-loves are the usual way we arrive at some degree of self-transcendence. But they can easily go in several directions like pure distraction or dissipation or deteriorate into libidinous liaisons and, therefore, become erotic. So, morally, there is probably some degree of ambiguity in them, to speak in general.

One of my misgivings about this second position comes from Ignatius Loyola's insight into his own humanity, which has enabled many to be clearer about theirs. His clarity came from his profound appreciation of the end to which we are called. Without a real appropriation of this, he insisted, it is easy to confuse an end and a means. "I must not subject and fit the end to the means, but the means to the end."[5] An experience of eros-love, looked at in the light of eternity, is really a means to our end of union with God. But it can be twisted and sanitized by claiming that the eros-love is one with that end without the warrant for making that claim. This is twisting God to serve our ends rather than serving God as our end by keeping means in the order of means. I am not saying that a relationship of love should ever be made a means in the mundane order of means and ends but vis-a-vis God it must be. Rationalizing a relationship by giving it a theological sheen can keep it from being examined for what it really is. Ever since Israel was disciplined for making a god of its own devising, humans have been prone to making idols.

A further reason for having misgivings about this second continuum position is the fact that the more satisfying the eros-love is, the more likely it will be fraught with ambiguity. In fact, the closer the eros-love gets to being "the best" of my relationships, the greater the possibility it has of usurping the place God is meant to have in our lives. It may well be that a given relationship is a "gift of God," but the proof of this will come over time, and the evidence will be that one's love of God has increased. One of the deepest ironies of "the gift of God" characterization of a given relationship is that its net result can often be that there is much less time for God and the things of God, which include care for others because more and more time is invested in the relationship.

It seems to me that one of the important tests of an eros-love is: who, if anyone, is excluded by it? Loving one another is at the heart of the gospel. And this love commandment has a command component to it. It is clearly meant to include those who are not naturally lovable, such as the stranger, the Lazarus outside the gate of my comfort zone, even the enemy. But in order to go that extra mile and to give that coat or to attend to the unattractive and undesirable, the eros-loves that are more naturally appealing must not preoccupy us to the point that we are unfree to obey this more difficult part of the love commandment. An eros-love that leaves us neighbor-numb is an eros-love that still hasn't passed the gospel test of self-transcendence.

A More Perfect Way

These considerations lead me to a third position. Having decided against the secularization of eros-loves in the first position and against the facile conflation of eros-loves with *agapē* in the second position, I want to argue for a third position, namely, that eros-loves are good but not yet good enough. They need the constant "work" of transformation by the energy of holiness, which is *agapē*-love. This third position is a transformationist one.

To explain this third position I know I must be clearer about the meaning of *agapē*-love. It is peculiar to God. Its point of origin is the Trinity itself, which is Trinity precisely because of this pure giving of "Father" to "Son," "Son" to "Father," these two to the third, "Spirit," and the "Spirit" to "Father and Son." I place quotation marks around these triune relations to underscore that there is an unfathomable mystery about this *agapē*-Love. Each of these Divine "Persons" is distinct precisely because of the poured-out character of the other two Persons. Their one nature is *agapē*. In brief, "God is love" (1 John 4:8). What would a person be like whose whole reality, whose whole existence is love poured out? The only human analogue I can think of that comes close to plumbing this way of being is ecstatic love, when the lover is so smitten by the beloved as to have virtually become the beloved. But what's deliriously wonderful about the little knowledge we have of God is that God doesn't keep this agapic love within the preserve of the Trinity but pours it out.

What does *agapē*-love have to do with eros-love? Catholic theology has usually explained this question in terms of the virtues, of *caritas,* in particular. The traditional understanding of the infused virtues of which *caritas* is one is that there is the outpoured (uncreated) *agapē*-love of God that infuses believers with the (created) three theological virtues. They are called theological virtues because they create the immediate possibility of bonds between the person and God that could not otherwise be forged. Nature alone could not create these bonds.

This third position contends that agapic love—which is the Spirit poured out and indwelling us—is given to effect not only our relationship with God but also our eros-loves. *Caritas,* the specific, created gift that the Spirit confers, is given in order to transform our eros-loves and complete them. *Agapē*-love, which is God's love for us, enables us through *caritas* in particular (though faith and hope are also presumed to be operative), to transform our eros-loves so that they are brought into an integrity in themselves. But also they are meant to have a sacramental effect in the sense of enabling one's mind and heart to love our friends in God and God in our friends. The transformation of our human loves is an ongoing process. Practice makes perfect. Once our human loves are brought into the field of energy of *agape/caritas,* which experientially is our relationship of friendship with Christ, then our loves will have integrity. Without the nexus, our love of God can plateau, become faint, even die.

Here again, notice how holiness is an already and a not-yet kind of a thing. As an already, it has been received. As a not-yet, it is always slightly ahead of us as an invitation and a possibility waiting to be housed. It is housed insofar as our eros-loves are suffused with the *agapē-caritas* field of energy. This field of force is given us to grow in friendship with God while our transformed eros-loves serve to deepen that friendship. Just as holiness is at best a work in progress, so also are our friendships in the Lord.

There is a form of prayer that is most congenial to the line of thought taken in this third theological position. It is Epiclesis (Spirit-invoking) prayer. Just as before the eucharistic consecration the priest prays the Epiclesis ("Let the Spirit come upon the gifts of bread and wine to make them holy that they might become for us the body and blood of Christ"), so also here the Christian can pray that the Spirit might come upon his or her eros-loves so that they might be increasingly refined in the fire of God's love. The prayer is that we might experience our friendships as friends in the Lord. This prayer is said to enable us to experience a friend as bread that feeds both our love of that friend and the eternal life that Eucharist nourishes in us. Surely God is glorified by this prayer and this kind of love.

One who is *caritas*-active is acting in a way that is humanly replicating the way the Trinity "acts" within itself. Concretely, as this virtue becomes habitual, one's eros-loves will begin to replicate the poured-out character of God's a*gapē*-love. With trinitarian a*gapē* as the source of this power, generosity, self-sacrifice, giving without counting the cost—all these qualities grow. Of course, this transformation of our loving is never complete or automatic. If one's life is centered on Jesus Christ as friend and not only friend but also Lord, that pearl of great price will transform everything about one's life, especially one's loves, each of which remains a pearl but of lesser price.

What is the difference between a relationship that is experienced as a merely immanent kind of thing, and one that is also open to the transcendent and, therefore, experienced as sacramental? The eyes of the two parties in the first case remain on one another, on the here and now. But in the second case, they relate to one another with God and the ways of God suffusing their mutuality. In the first case the dynamic is confined to us or to me and him, or me and her; in the second case the dynamic is a threesome in the sense that the relationship operates in an awareness of the horizon of God. In the first case the Giver of the gift and the gift are separate; in the second case the Giver is not detached from the gift. If the eros-love is experienced as a gift God has given, then two disciplines can kick in. One of these is inclusion. The eros-love is always in some manner included in one's life-orienting love of God. And with the ongoing inclusion, there is the second discipline, that of obedience. This means that I do not have anything that my will generates in the relationship that is at variance with or separate from the obedience my will has to God in other aspects of my life. And these are not disciplines exercised in isolation but, with varying degrees of explicitness, are also practiced by my friends in the Lord. We abide in the love of the Vine and are aware of the command/promise that "if you remain in me and my words remain in you, ask for whatever you want and it will be done for you. By this is my Father glorified, that you bear much fruit" (John 15:7–8).

But this reflection would be incomplete without including others' needs. Friendships in the Lord cannot be unavailable to neighbor. Jesus as the enfleshment of *agapē*-love goes from his supper with his friends to his death, not only for those he called his friends, but for those who crucified him. If my eros-loves do not leave me free to love the stranger, the chances are poor that the transformation being described here is taking place.

Before leaving this matter I want to point to a pericope in John that contains much wisdom about eros-loves. It seems to me to contain the key attitude necessary for their transformation. The context is the irritation and competitive spirit beginning to develop in John the Baptist's disciples because they saw Jesus of Nazareth winning over the Baptist's clientele. They complained to John that Jesus "is baptizing and everyone is coming to him" (John 3:26). John's response is enlightening. "The one who has the bride is the bridegroom; the best man, who stands and listens for him, rejoices greatly at the bridegroom's voice" (John 3:29). These are certainly strong images; one could even describe them as "third-party love words." John the Baptist is locating himself in the category of one who is removed from the tryst between bride and groom but who assists in its intimacy, as a best man would do. The attitude and the norm voiced by John: "This joy of mine has been made complete. He must increase; I must decrease" (John 3:29–30). What could be more clear about the right order of a Christian's eros-loves? Even when that eros-love becomes as intimate as a marriage, the real spouse of one's own spouse is Christ. And this is all the more true when the eros-love is far short of marriage: the real spouse of my friend is Christ. Relationships that distract from this order are not being transformed in the direction cited by John's principle here: "He must increase; I must decrease." When the bridegroom increases through our eros-loves, God is glorified.

The Glory of God

I deliberately chose two everyday things that are part of the lives of all of us, the news and our relationships, to show concretely how from the holiness we have in Christ, God is glorified through the eros with which God has scripted our natures. The icon of the unity between human eros and the holiness of God is always the person of Christ. If his unique (hypostatic) union of his two natures had been reserved to his own person we would never be able to hold in fruitful tension the eros and *agapē* that he knew and we participate in by reason of the Spirit gift. But we do know this fruitful tension, and by abiding in love, God's holiness is housed in us, and God is glorified.

This chapter has moved concern about our holiness off of what could be dead center, namely, the self as holy or our growing in holiness. By looking at two of the specific things in the lives of all of us, I suggested that our holiness, such as it is, should be attentive to God's glory so that one's life is a praise of God. I now want to introduce the reader to a woman who has been important in confirming my heart and mind to move in this direction. Elizabeth Catez was born in 1880 in Bourges, France. But the name given her in religious life, to her great delight, was Elizabeth of the Trinity. She learned in her short life span of twenty-six years that her life was to be lived as "a praise of His glory." Her life and this way of seeing it have impressed me as a valuable way, maybe the best way, to understand the call to holiness that Vatican Council II six decades later has urged. Blessed Elizabeth's understanding of holiness as the praise of God's glory decenters the issue from the self and one's holiness, which could become rather precious if it were not to develop in this further direction.

We have Hans Urs von Balthasar to thank for elaborating to the church the significance of Elizabeth's special charism. In poring over her writings, he realized that she was clear evidence for his overall theological insight that to be a saint is to be a servant of the Holy Spirit. He considered a saint to be one who has received a special mission for the church to incarnate and bear witness to the people of God to some aspect of the immeasurable richness of Christ. "The mission that each individual receives contains within itself the form of sanctity that has been granted to him/her and is required of them."[6] He sees an individual's particular mission or charism as both the person's "appropriate capacity for sanctity" and, at the same time, "essentially social," that is, for the upbuilding of the rest of us (Ibid.). "For each Christian, God has an idea . . . unique and personal," the fulfillment of which "will be their sanctity." He describes this idea as first "secreted in God" but which should become the "individual law" of the person as they come to know it (Ibid., 21).

Elizabeth became clear about her charism. I am "a bottomless abyss into which God spreads himself and pours himself forth" (Ibid., 465). (I will retain her politically incorrect language since it's hers.) Almost as if she were a bystander, she felt

herself as one in whom "the Divine Being [is free] to satiate his
hunger to give all he is" so that her whole person could become
a "praise of his glory" (Ibid., 466). She experienced herself as
being transformed by God into Christ so that "when the Father
leans over this soul (me) he feels the same as when he sees his
Son . . . then he thrills in his paternal heart and determines to
crown his work—to glorify her, to transport her into his Kingdom so she can sing the praise of his glory in endless eternities
there" (Ibid., 467). This may all seem so grand as to leave the rest
of us sinners so far behind that we disidentify with her. However,
she learned to own what she considered her very serious weaknesses, but realized that being a praise of God's glory meant that
she should not dwell on them. "It is the weakest, indeed, the
most guilty soul who has the best grounds for hope, and this act
by which she surrenders herself and throws herself into the arms
of God, glorifies him more and gives him more joy than all her
introspections and examinations of conscience, which only
cause her to dwell on her weakness" (Ibid., 415). This is an
important realization without which we will not come to know
that we, who are also the guilty, are to be "co-heirs of his
[Christ's] inheritance of glory" (Ibid., 415). It seemed to her that
what was happening to her was "the dream of the Creator [for
all] . . . to see himself in his creature, to see his perfections, his
full beauty, reflected as in clear, spotless crystal: Is that not a kind
of extension of his own glory?" (Ibid., 447).

   She was enough of a modern to be conscious of her consciousness. She learned by reflection how her consciousness could
be either useless or helpful in living out her calling. Someone who
is "preoccupied with her own feeling and useless thoughts, who
clings to all sorts of desires—such a soul dissipates her powers"
(Ibid., 446). She likened the useless use of consciousness to being
an instrument so out of tune that "when the Master strokes it, he

can coax no divine tones from it," so dissonant is it. Consequently, by having one's consciousness all over the place, she can be no perfect praise of glory for unity does not reign in her." Then, instead of a unitary consciousness, "she has to devote herself constantly to collecting the strings of her instrument that have been scattered in all directions" (Ibid.). She specialized, so to speak, not in trying to have a unitary consciousness but "in no longer being self-preoccupied . . . the saints are those who are forever forgetting themselves" (Ibid., 448). In her last retreat she referred to herself not as Elizabeth of the Trinity but as Elizabeth the Vanishing (Ibid.). It's not that she did not have mood swings but that she did not count them as significant. "Don't let it bother you that you are either passionately enthused or depressed—it is the law of this world that we waver between one emotional state and another. You must simply trust the fact that he never changes, that he is always bending over you in kindness" (Ibid., 450). So when she looked into her consciousness, she was able to see its deeper horizon and realize that "she carries within herself a little heaven where the God of love has set up housekeeping" (Ibid.). She became aware and amazed that "the Trinity loves to gaze on its beauty in my soul" and that, therefore, everything she did was to be done "under the gaze" of the divine Persons (Ibid., 463). Is this narcissism or a charism for all the church to grow in its awareness of the doctrine of the divine indwelling?

Her consciousness of and acceptance of her particular charism can be seen in her petitionary prayer: "Consecrate your child to almighty love so that love might reshape her into the praise of your glory" (Ibid., 479). The feast of the Holy Trinity was her favorite day of all the year. On one of those feast days she wrote: "Never before have I grasped so well the mystery and the entire calling that lies within my name." Part of a poem she wrote on this occasion is as follows:

The Trinity drew me into an embrace,
I found in its abyss my landing.
No one can carry me back to shore,
For I range freely in boundlessness,
No bars block my recreation,
My endless life lives in the Holy Three. (Ibid., 478)

"How can one glorify God? . . . [by your seeing] each pain as
well as each joy as having come directly from him, [as a result]
your life will be an unbroken communion, because everything will
become a sacrament that gives God to you." She continues,
"things, in a sense, are only the rays of his love. Now you see how
you can glorify him in these scarcely bearable situations of suffering and exhaustion"(Ibid., 455). In 1906, Elizabeth died of a
painful illness, Addison's disease, and was beatified by Pope John
Paul II on November 25, 1984.

She was not given to theologizing, having never studied theology, yet she was able to see and name the work of the Holy Spirit
that was going on in her. That work was to complete God's plan
for her, of being conformed to the image of the Son. She experienced God as both a "consuming fire" that was refining what was
not of God in her while also giving her a great desire to "tumble
into the flaming hearth, which is the Holy Spirit himself, the very
love that binds the Father and his Word together in the Trinity"
(Ibid., 473). Her consciousness became so identified with the
Trinity that she experienced in herself what she dared to call an
"equality with God," even a "deification." At the same time she was
utterly aware that there was another equally true side of herself—
her own nothingness and the humiliation of it. Hence she can
speak of a "double abyss: God's boundlessness and (my/our) own
nothingness" (Ibid., 475).

What proved to be the life-changing text for her was Paul's letter to the Ephesians: "We were also chosen, destined in accord with the purpose of the One who accomplished all things according to the intention of his will, so that we might exist for the praise of his glory" (Eph. 1:11–12). She housed this mystery both as her own and as true of all those who are in Christ. It is from this text that many of her personal reflections about her mission derive. She can be dismissed as having no relevance for the rest of us if we categorize her as having a contemplative vocation and, therefore, beyond the pale of what is germane for us active types. That would be an unfortunate dismissal of her for two reasons. First, she saw her own mission as not only contemplative and vertical, if we can trivialize it by such a spatial image, but also as apostolic and horizontal, to complete the image. She saw her life as a service of the church and herself as having a continuing work on earth even after her death. (In this she was similar to the Little Flower, who was a contemporary of hers.) I don't know what this means except that with the clear testimony she gave about the significance of a life lived for the praise of God's glory, we can all be enriched by it. But the second reason she should not be dismissed will be elaborated on in the next two chapters, namely, that God is glorified when each person comes to be "fully alive." *Gloria Dei vivens homo* is the saying for which we remember St. Irenaeus, a second-century bishop of Gaul. The glory of God is human beings fully alive. How pleased God must be that the fuller life or flourishing of all persons is now, in the twentieth and twenty-first centuries, being accorded a place of such importance.

6

Solidarity and Holiness

IF HOLINESS IS BEST STRIVEN for by being focused on God's glory, and if God is glorified by "a human fully alive," what follows from this? Individuals alive at all levels of their potential, obviously. Less obvious, and the subject of this chapter, are the solidarities that actualize the potentials of individuals. An Elizabeth of the Trinity is inexplicable without the solidarities of her family and religious community. As I hope to show, solidarity is an aspiration and an ideal. It is also a virtue and a large part of the explanation for individuals of heroic virtue and their high ideals. Further, solidarity is the ingredient that will make "the commons" good and the good more common.

History

Solidarities are intrinsic to holiness. What do I mean by solidarity? For starters we can use the definition of Pope John Paul II, who describes solidarity as "a firm and persevering determination to commit oneself to the common good . . . i.e., to the good of all and of each individual because we are really responsible for all" (*Sollicitudo Rei Socialis,* 38). The first insights about the importance of solidarity were developed in ancient Greece. The city-state and its commons were seen to be the place for human flourishing. Greek personhood was social. One's virtues were those of a citizen of the *polis,* the city. Solidarity was not named a virtue by the Greeks since it was within that political ambit that all the citizens' virtues operated. Nor was the common good singled out as a specification of the good, since it was the primary good all were supposedly in concert to attain. Striving for a private good independently of the good of the community at that point in human history would have been considered a misunderstanding of the good and a sign of moral pathology.

But in ancient Israel, as noted in chapter 2, holiness was a call to solidarity, to a people who were to be a people under the God who had called them out of darkness and oppression into the marvelous light of harmony with one another under God. The evidence of having heard and responded to the call was their solidarity as a people. The people became a holy people not one by one or vertically but horizontally, so to speak. The split between Israel and Christianity in some ways marred this whole-people understanding of holiness. Often Christians' understanding of their relationship with the risen Jesus only added to this individuated image of holiness, as I hope to show. Further, there are any number of sociological accounts of how the self emerged in modern times, how it exited the primary communities of the previous centuries and the traditions that bound the self to its solidarities. In these earlier centuries, "I's" emerged much more slowly from the "we's" of which they were a part and seldom completely disjoined from them. Finally, modern political liberalism makes solidarities problematic, infrequent, and thin because individual citizens are busy striving for their particular good. Although very sketchy, these vignettes give one a sense of the difficulty solidarity is having in modern times.

Modern Catholic social teaching insists on linking the good of the person with the community's good. The 1931 encyclical *Quadragesimo Anno* of Pope Pius XI began the march of solidarity into Catholic consciousness in modern times. In 1961 Pope John XXIII examined solidarity in terms of the common good, which he defined as "the sum total of conditions of social living whereby persons are enabled more fully and readily to achieve their own perfection" (*Mater et Magistra*, 65). For him, the common good would be guaranteed when there was a balance between personal rights and communal responsibilities. Vatican Council II insisted on the importance of members of society contributing to the common good in accord with their own abilities and others' needs (*Gaudium et Spes*, 30). The result would make the whole of the citizenry the beneficiaries of the commonweal that was produced by each one's contributing his or her part.

The Solidarity Pope

But the strongest proponent of solidarity in modern times has been the present pope, John Paul II. He lifts it to the stature of a virtue, one that is on a par with the virtue of *caritas*. It is likened by him to a kind of social charity. It is also akin to social justice but with an emphasis on the "total gratuity" of love as its motivating force. It is not content with the bonds we have with one another by reason of our common human nature. Accepting and assuming these, it seeks by actions to forge deeper bonds for the sake of advancing and upbuilding the common good, which is the good of all and each. The self-transcendence required to think and act and live this way is already on the road to losing one's life for others and thereby finding it as the gospel prescribes. In a word, holiness.

John Paul sees solidarity as a manifestation of God's own love, which is infused as a theological virtue enabling the one who receives it to live a life of friendship with God. So, before it becomes a moral/civic virtue, it is an unmerited gift from God. John Paul has connected two previously unconnected pieces. Not only does the infused energy of *caritas* enable friendship with God, it also enables civic friendship, as Aristotle would call it. The best model of the exercise of this virtue of *caritas*-solidarity, as with any other Christian virtue, is the person of Jesus. When we think of the solidarities he formed, there were the Twelve, the seventy-two, the eating and drinking he did with tax collectors and sinners—something considered extemely inappropriate by those whose highly selective companionship served to reinforce their moral elitism. For Pope John Paul II, these new emphases about solidarity as a gift and a virtue do not come from speculating. He saw the social force for good that a cohesive union of minds and hearts could generate in his own native Poland, beginning in the Gdansk shipyards and ending with the toppling of totalitarian Polish Communism.

The Catholic understanding of holiness will never be the same after this present pope's treatment of solidarity as *caritas* or *caritas* as solidarity. John Paul's solidarity excludes no one except those who choose to exclude themselves, like the party bosses in his native Poland. It recognizes the fact that every one of our neighbors is fundamentally equal to us, as we are to them, because each of us is to be "a praise of his glory" by being "fully alive." All people are "living images of God redeemed by the blood of Jesus Christ and placed under the permanent action of the Holy Spirit," even though most are unaware of their stature.[1]

It is interesting to follow the progression taken by this pope on this subject, a progression we would all be well advised to undertake. His first reflections on it were in his encyclical on Human Work (*Laborem Exercens*, 1981). Solidarity is presented there as a worker phenomenon. Workers, reacting against dehumanizing conditions of work, boldly began to create communities of solidarity in his native land. Usually these were conceived of as unions that sought to redress the systems of injustice that exploited them. Six years later in his encyclical *Sollicitudo Rei Socialis*, John Paul brought greater depth and breadth to the subject. He speaks there of the "moral value of the growing awareness of interdependence among individuals and nations." This awareness leads people "to feel personally affected by the injustices and violations of human rights" committed across the globe in lands they will never visit. This knowledge evokes a transformation in consciousness of our interdependence with each other. This consciousness of interdependence has a "moral connotation" because it is so much more than "a feeling of vague compassion or shallow distress at the misfortunes of so many people both near and afar" (Ibid., 38). A conscious awareness of our interdependence with one another becomes a virtue when it grows into "a firm and persevering determination to commit oneself to the common good" (Ibid., 38). This determination matures when there is "the solid conviction" that the dire conditions people face are due to "structures of sin," which can be dismantled because they were constructed. "Presupposing the help of divine grace, by a diametrically opposed attitude" entails "losing oneself for the sake of the other and serving him or her rather than relating to the other from a position of personal advantage or self-interest or indifference" (Ibid., 38).

This other in the relation of solidarity can be a person, a people, or a nation. These are experienced as relations of interdependence that have been forged from two convictions. One is "that the goods of creation are meant for all." The second is that the other is meant "to be a sharer, on a par with ourselves, in the banquet of life to which all are equally invited by God" (Ibid., 39). In the next section of the encyclical, the pope, aware of the strong horizontal direction in which he is calling the church, roots solidarity in the life of the Trinity. The Holy Spirit, the pope is certain, would imbue Christians with a vision of the world that is to be aligned with "the supreme model of unity which is a reflection of the intimate life of God, one God in three Persons" (Ibid., 40). This vision of the trinitarian communion "is the soul of the church's mission to be a sacrament" (Ibid., 40).

Widening Solidarity

The pope goes even further with his category of "the other" with which we are in solidarity. In *Sollicitudo,* he speaks of the limits of the available resources in our world and the need to respect the integrity and cycles of nature (Ibid., 26). Are we not also in a solidarity with these cycles of nature, and is not attention to the integrity of nonrenewable resources our responsibility? Under the section called "Authentic Human Development," the pope speaks of its moral dimension, which includes our need to have "respect for the beings which constitute the natural world." In using these he teaches, "one must take into account the nature of each being and its mutual connection in an ordered system which is precisely the cosmos" (Ibid., 34). Our solidarity must be with this web of life of the total earth community in which we are immediately enfolded.

Many voices are being raised to have the church become even "greener" about our relationship with earth and its endangered life cycles and ecosystem. One of these voices has eloquently observed that "solidarity among people has no basis unless it is equally grounded in a solidarity with nature. The earth herself is calling forth this new awareness, this new sense of each and all belonging to a whole."[2] Once human identity, personal identity, takes the solidarity route, it seems a wider vision of wholeness beckons us to ever wider circles. The trinitarian model of solidarity is strengthened by this vision of wholeness, which grounds human holiness with our life on earth and with the things of earth and our inextricable kinship with them.

I have appreciated a number of the things Elizabeth Johnson has written on this subject. She stresses the fact that we are all kin in one mutually interdependent community of life. "The natural world has given birth to all living things and sustains us all. It is the matrix of our origin, growth and fulfillment."[3] Unfortunately, two biases tend to distract us from this vision of wholeness. The first bias is the traditional way we see our relationship to nature as stewards. Stewardship has us see ourselves as responsible for being caretakers and guardians of the earth and its creatures. But she sees the inadequacy of this idea because "it misses the crucial aspect of human dependence upon that which we steward." The second bias regards our consciousness. Johnson writes: "Human consciousness is in continuity with the energy of matter stretching back through galactic ages to the Big Bang, being a special, intense form of this energy." I'm sure the understanding of the relationship of the physical brain to human consciousness is still in its infancy, but Johnson relates the evolution of the brain to "ever more powerful forms of spirit; matter, alive with energy, evolves to spirit" (Ibid., 31, 37).

Without fully understanding this latter move, I believe wisdom is in the vision of wholeness laid out here. It takes our interdependence beyond the interhuman and sees it organically, appreciating our undeniable interdependence on the things of earth. They and we are "intrinsically related as companions in a community of life" (Ibid., 37). *Homo sapiens* has emerged from earth genetically but continues to be submerged in it for its nurturing and continuance. Thomas Berry, who has been one of the most eloquent spokesmen for this kind of interdependence, has elaborated it metaphorically. He sees the human species as part of a great journey, the journey of primordial matter through its marvelous sequence of transformations in the stars, in the earth, in living creatures, in human consciousness.[4] This wider vision of solidarity, it seems to me, makes Prometheus look quaint, since not only fire but also water and air and matter and the quintessence were already all around him. He needn't have stolen fire from heaven.

Translated: holiness is very much wrapped up with that with which we interdepend. We can understand our dependence on God in more tangible ways and our responsibility about caring for these things God has made in more immediate terms by developing this ecological awareness. With this awareness, we can re-enchant the things of earth and all the life that earth teems with. We are convicted of the disenchantment we have been guilty of for centuries by our utilitarian, pragmatic, and increasingly coarse use of the things with which God has been loving us all our life long.

Theological Ecology

The previous section takes into account "the dust factor," both the fact that we were formed "out of the clay of the ground" (Gen. 2:7) and that earth, therefore, does not belong to humans but humans belong to earth. It has always been too easy to succumb to the "Platonic temptation" that denies we are formed out of the matter of the universe. When we succumb to this temptation, holiness becomes a trip past the materiality of our own being and the whole biosphere and out into a spiritual beyond. Rahner was not doing ecological theology but ontology and theological anthropology when he refused to see the spirit and matter of a human being separately or as two elements extrinsically related one to the other. He insisted on their being "the realization and accomplishment of one essence."[5] While the human being is "radically distinct from any animal," the human is distinct "in such a fashion that he [sic] carries with him the whole inheritance of his biological prehistory into the realm of his existence remote from animals."[6]

We are one with nature and its materiality by reason not only of our beginning but also of our end. The earth's destiny and that of humans are of a piece. As body/spirit, we need materiality to realize our purposes and destiny. So, also, nature needs us to realize its destiny. Our being inextricable from the rest of creation was never articulated better than by Paul's classic statement on the subject. "Creation awaits with eager expectation the revelation of the children of God; for creation was made subject to futility, not of its own accord but because of the one who subjected it, in hope that creation itself would be set free from slavery to corruption and share in the glorious freedom of the children of God" (Rom. 8:19–21).

Nature is not a neutral stage on which we humans work out our salvation. "The climax of salvation history is not the detachment from the world of man as a spirit in order to come to God, but the descending and irreversible entrance of God into the world, the coming of the divine Logos in the flesh, the taking up of the material world so that it itself becomes a permanent reality of God in which God in his Logos expresses himself to us forever" (Ibid., 160). What is brought to holiness is what was created from matter, not something spiritualized beyond its materiality. Matter is not the raw material for our holiness but intrinsic to it. "Rahner insists that the order of creation and the order of salvation *(ordo salutis)* must be considered as a dialectical unity. . . . The order of creation is precisely that which passes into the order of salvation and the order of salvation is the consummation of the order of creation."[7] Consistent with this line of thinking, the kingdom of God is then seen not simply as a moral order but a cosmic order as well. God is and has been a Creator God and has been misunderstood when construed as a deistic, a-cosmic kind of deity. Gone forever with this realization are the dualism and mental construct of a heaven as a place for souls to flee to.

Our understanding of the theology of ecology is incomplete at this point. We must ask what the incarnation can tell us about our solidarity with the material realities commented on above. It tells us of the depth of God's commitment to the world. "God so loved the world that he gave his only Son . . . [not to] condemn the world, but that the world might be saved through him" (John 3:16–17). From the incarnation on, it has been particularly unenlightened or uninformed to construe human beings apart from God's love. But an a-cosmic way of thinking about God also flies in the face of the incarnation. For Karl Rahner, the incarnation was not simply the central event in human history. It was a cosmic event, an event that is central to the history of the entire cosmos.[8]

The resurrection of the body is a symbol that applies to the destiny of the whole cosmos. "In the glorified body of Jesus there is the beginning of the transfiguration of the world as an ontologically interconnected occurrence . . . a beginning in which the destiny of the world is already in principle decided and has already begun. . . . The world as a whole flows into his Resurrection and into the transfiguration of his body."[9]

Communion and Solidarity

Of all the solidarities that are possible to us humans, there is one that merits a greater attention than all the rest. It is the solidarity that can be forged only by the Holy Spirit. To understand this particular kind of solidarity, we must first reflect on the three divine Persons, since they are the source and ground of this kind of solidarity. The Trinity is a *communio personarum,* as Pope John Paul has reminded the faithful again and again.[10] By referring to the Trinity in terms of a "communion" of Persons, the pope is using a term the Christian tradition has perennially used for the solidarities that God alone can forge. The Greek term for this kind of solidarity is *koinōnia,* which means communion or, more weakly, fellowship. So, between human beings the Spirit is able to create a communion that has its ground in no less a reality than the communion of the three divine Persons themselves.

The term *koinōnia,* or communion, is a favorite one of Paul. He uses it to inform those who have come together in faith in Christ that their bond is a *koinōnia* that has the Spirit as its author (1 Cor. 1:9). His prayer for all his churches is: "The grace of the Lord Jesus Christ and the love of God and the fellowship [*koinōnia*] of the holy Spirit be with you all" (2 Cor. 13:13). Only the Spirit can make a bond that has an eternity to it. Only the Spirit can make a bond that is both horizontal, that is, between people, and vertical, that is, between God and person and the people. It is toward this form of communion that all other solidarities are vectored, even though knowledge of this finality would be fairly rare. The irreducible diversity within the Trinity of divine Persons should be a constant reminder that the finality of all solidarities would not be homogeneity but unity in diversity.

What does their divine ground tell us about solidarities? That while each is of great importance to those who benefit from it, the agenda of God would seem to point them toward a communion of solidarities. A communion of solidarities would not eradicate or homogenize a particular solidarity, but its coherence would have to be considered partial and incomplete vis-à-vis other solidarities. To make this less abstract, let me use the example of the Christian churches, since I believe that their ecumenical efforts are the bellwether of other kinds of solidarities.

Twenty years after Vatican II, an international synod was convoked to evaluate that extraordinary event. It baldly stated that "the ecclesiology of communion is the central and fundamental idea in the council's documents."[11] The church is only as real as it is local. But the church is only as true to its sources as it is one in all of its instantiations. "I pray, . . . Father, . . . that they may also be in us, that the world may believe that you sent me" (John 17:20–21). A communion of the churches is what the council envisioned as key to the future agenda of the churches. What I am suggesting here is that a passion for that *telos* can unleash a passion for the holiness of God, which is blocked at all the points where partial solidarities stand against other partial solidarities, each content to remain incomplete, without even adverting to their incompleteness and the price they pay for their insularity.

But the Spirit "blows where it wills" (John 3:8) and, therefore, is not limited by insular solidarities, nor is it putting all other solidarities on hold till the churches get their act together. The Spirit is at work in the heart of every person, not only those who believe in God or who know the mystery of God as trinitarian. The council's insight into the scope of the work of the Spirit is breathtaking: "Humanity is continually being stirred by the Spirit of God. . . . People will always want to know what meaning to give to their lives, their activity and their death" (*Gaudium et Spes*, 41). The Spirit is always "animating, purifying and reinforcing the noble aspirations which drive the human family to make its life

one that is more human and to direct the whole earth to this end"
(Ibid., 38). All of which is to say that aspirations for solidarities
not yet realized and the developing insights into the need for solidarities not even imagined at present—these are the work and
agenda of the Spirit of holiness. Our ability to give God glory will
be proportionate to our insight into and action on behalf of the solidarities of which we are part and of which we are the beneficiaries.

7

The Glory of God
in the Larger Society

IN THE PREVIOUS TWO CHAPTERS we have looked at solidarities and their relations to holiness. We have also looked at how we can give glory to God through some of the things that swell the agendas of our daily lives, and live a life "for the praise of his glory." In this final chapter I want to focus on our civic relationships. We interact and connect with others, our fellow citizens, all the day long, though more impersonally and impartially than we do in our eros relationships. What does holiness have to do with these civic relationships? Does holiness include this wider rim of our interactions? Does the call to holiness encompass our lives as citizens? If it does, holiness must be political in the sense that it must extend out to the *polis,* the life of the city, even to the nations. I will contend in this chapter that if it does not, our understanding of holiness is shortsighted, and the "human city" is being shortchanged. This is a complex matter. I will confine myself here to one aspect of it, the issue of human rights.

I can vividly recall when I got curious about the link between holiness and human rights. It was at the International Human

Rights Conference in Vienna, Austria, in June 1993. It was the first time the United Nations had convoked an international conference on human rights for its signatory nations since the signing of the Universal Declaration of Human Rights forty-five years before. Three moments in that unforgettable weeklong experience stand out. One was with Burmese students who had been expelled from Burma (Myanmar) because of their unrelenting opposition to the junta that had refused to acknowledge the will of the people as expressed by their vote. In listening to the students I wondered, what greater love could there be than to lay down one's life for one's people, as they were doing? Here was holiness. Was it a secular holiness? I seriously doubted that was a correct description of it, or of them, for reasons I will elaborate shortly. A second moment was with a Sudanese woman who described the profound humiliation of African women who are forced into female circumcision. Forgoing all her own interests, she was spending all her personal resources trying to have that barbarism outlawed. She unforgettably exclaimed that if the pain of these millions of mutilated women were to be emitted simultaneously "it would shatter the earth." Hers was a total response to the violation of her female neighbors. Was this not heroic virtue? Could sanctity be more heroic than this? Finally, the Thursday of that week was the Feast of St. Thomas More, one of my favorite saints. That morning I spoke at length with one of the students who had to flee China because of his known leadership at the Tiananmen Square demonstrations. He and other "enemies of the state" had set up a New York–based Center for Human Rights in China. His passion for his people's freedom was touching. Would God see his *non serviam* to the Communist party any differently than the canonized More's to the king who executed him?

I think it would be hard to ignore human rights and give glory to God or to give a complete account of what holiness in the

present age entails. Human rights have become a particularly crucial feature of the quality of our lives together on planet Earth.
Here I will seek to demonstrate that any aspiration to holiness or
to the praise of God's glory cannot be fully realized without a
commitment to the rights of those with whom we are associated.

A Brief History

To make that case, a brief excursion back into history will help. All
during the Enlightenment a rights morality was beginning to
develop. But it burst from the backwaters of philosophers' minds
into the consciousness of whole nations with the words of
Thomas Jefferson: "All men are created equal and endowed by
their Creator with certain inalienable rights." Inalienable, meaning
they are written into the fabric of every person's social existence.
At its simplest, having rights means I can make a moral claim on
others, and they on me, for whatever action is necessary for our
respective well-being. This simple idea grounds our moral interdependence on one another. What is entailed specifically in living
out this interdependence is what human rights documents,
treaties, agreements, and laws seek to elaborate. A rights morality
would claim that to ignore this interdependence, or to violate it,
or to not take some responsibility for meeting others' claims, is to
live an immoral or morally immature life or a vincibly ignorant
one. Conversely, to live a life attuned to, concerned for, and taking
some degree of responsibility for others' rights is an essential condition for living morally, even though the category of human
rights might not be explicit in the mind of the moral agent. If concern for the rights of the other affects one's agenda with regular-
ity, one is living altruistically at the very least.

It wasn't the faiths as such, nor Enlightenment reason, that fomented the rallying cry for human rights in this century. It was a planetwide revulsion at the organized killing of so many by so many (estimates are that 150 million people have been killed in the twentieth century by other people, not including abortions). World War II, the atomic bomb, the obliteration of whole cities by saturation bombing, the Holocaust in particular—by mid-century, all these generated such an experience of horror about how human life had become appallingly cheap, that the urgency to do something finally produced action. The response of the whole world to the slaughter of innocent human beings was a cry of No! that reached high heaven. God, I believe, heard this cry the same way the cry of the Israelites was heard when it was emitted in Egypt. God's response to the Egyptians was the Exodus, followed by the Sinai commandments. And God's response to the horrors of World War II was the creation in 1945 of the United Nations, followed by its charter document, the Universal Declaration of Human Rights, in 1948. Who but God could have engineered so many wills to coalesce in this first virtually unanimous agreement on a moral category, human rights, that the world had ever arrived at?

The genius of a rights morality is that it creates virtually universal moral standards for critiquing the practices and policies of both individuals and nations. It gives individuals, groups, and nations a chance to have their cases heard at the bar of local, national, and international opinion and attract attention and action to their claims. This is the most promising way the human race has ever had of generating the moral authority to respond to abuses that previously were swept under the rug. This is why Boutros Boutros-Ghali, the former secretary-general of the United Nations, could observe that human rights are fast becoming the "ultimate norm of politics."[1] The victims of abuse can now argue for their rights with a trump card, whereas before they had been dealt no cards at all.

Any citizen of the United States who lived through the civil rights revolution of the 1960s would know the power of human rights. Internationally, the two most extraordinary examples of the power of human rights to overthrow the evils of the entrenched political systems are the relatively bloodless overthrow of the totalitarian Soviet Union between 1989 and 1991 and, in virtually the same years with the same nonbloody process, the destruction of the evil apartheid system in South Africa. Recall the thrilling success stories in these events. Had it not been for the Helsinki Watch dissidents in the Soviet Union (Andrei Sakharov, Anatoly Sharansky, and others; 1975 ff.), Solidarity in Poland (Lech Walesa and others; 1976 ff.), and the Velvet Revolution led by Vaclav Havel and others in Czechoslovakia (1977 ff.), all feeding data to the West, especially to the U.S. State Department, the Soviet system would not have fallen—at least not without much bloodshed. But these are instances of courageous individuals and nongovernmental organizations (NGOs) working with internationally like-minded groups and sympathetic nations like our own, all of them insisting on stopping the violation of persons and standing up for their inviolability. In the case of South Africa, Nelson Mandela's African National Congress was the knife that cut through the thicket of apartheid. But it would not have been successful without much outside pressure and assistance from NGOs such as the American Committee on Africa.

As in our own civil rights movement, the starkly simple issue these different forms of protest were forcing to the surface for resolute action was this: What is due a human being *qua* human being? What do we owe one another, given each one's dignity as human? In the bright light of day, it was obvious to all that what was due one another were the conditions necessary for human dignity. Yet it was often not being accorded them. Those who found the situation intolerable could now win out over those who wanted to look the other way. Although the violence of people against people continues, think of the degree of difficulty we would be in internationally had this moral standard about human dignity not been set since 1948. We would have reverted to a dark past of long ago, with totalitarian regimes doing unconscionable things to their people with impunity, with one generation's violence fomenting the next generation's violent retribution.

But a rights morality is a fragile victory because the theory necessary for undergirding human rights is not agreed on. The initial framers of the Universal Declaration on Human Rights were almost immediately aware that they would not be able to reach an agreement on the theory or foundation undergirding them. They agreed not to try to hammer one out since, at that time, in the aftermath of World War II and the worldwide shock at the human capacity for brutality, the declaration was deemed urgent. The framers hoped the theory could catch up with the practice down the line, but the theory has never caught up in an agreed-upon way. In its stead the rhetoric of rights is being used to proliferate rights beyond their initial rationale. Rights are all too often being argued for and promoted in a highly selective way. Conflicts over rights are becoming almost as frequent as rights claims. At the macro-level, for example, collectivist and socialist countries are still quite hostile to the idea of civil or political rights, while capitalist countries continue to deny that their citizens have social and economic rights. (Civil and political rights create the conditions of freedom; social and economic rights create the material conditions for human dignity. No country has as yet officially specified the right to unpolluted air, water, soil, and vegetation.) The U.N. Declaration was universal; the theory behind it is not. This has seriously endangered the moral heft that rights have needed, since political opportunism or selective interests are all too often behind their claim and promotion—or so the unconvinced believe.

Rights' Roots

I may have painted myself into a corner by now. I have claimed that the political is an essential component of holiness and, even more specifically, that without taking the measure of myself and others in terms of rights, our conception of holiness is truncated. But having said that, I have found that the idea of human rights is seriously thin at the point of an agreed-upon theoretical base. How can I get out of the corner? I believe that the Catholic Church has acquitted itself well in supplying a universal theoretical base for human rights. The church has complemented its acceptance of a rights morality with the moral foundation necessary for making the large claims about its importance that I have enunciated here. If a consensus cannot be reached concerning the foundation for this first universally agreed-upon moral category, there is every reason to believe that human rights claims will become more and more a source of conflict rather than of harmony in relationships near and far. This foundation is called natural law, a law that is as universal as the existence of human nature.

Recent church history needs to be recalled. The church was very late in coming to see the promise of a rights morality. In fact, for centuries the church had marched under a different banner, that "error [about doctrine or morals] has no rights." Since the church "had the truth," its leaders felt obliged to constrain or persecute or excommunicate those judged to be in error, notwithstanding the fact that the deviants were usually acting out of a

conviction of conscience. The church's position was, in effect, that
an erroneous conscience could be punished. The Inquisition is
still the most obvious historical evidence of that insular, immature
stage in the church's moral insight.

The Holy Spirit, as usual, would not leave matters as they
were. Two figures and one event were catalytic in turning the
church around about this subject. John Courtney Murray, S.J., is
deservedly legendary for sorting out the American experience
about religious freedom and freedom of conscience and making
his insights about these inalienable human rights available to the
universal church. Pope John XXIII and his encyclical *Pacem in Terris* (1963) superseded the previous history of the church on
human rights and brought it up to speed with the U.N. Declaration of Human Rights with the help of the work done by Murray
and others. Finally, Vatican II, particularly in its Declaration on
Religious Freedom *(Dignitatis Humanae),* definitively ended the
church's cold war with rights by adding this dimension to its
understanding of morality. (Needless to say, the church had been
consistently outstanding in practice in its long history for
responding to the claims and needs of others. These needs, however, were seldom voiced or responded to in terms of their human
rights, since the understanding of them had not advanced far
enough in either the church or the world to have the currency in
moral thought they now enjoy.)

Once it "bought" rights, the church's long moral tradition
was able to add something the United Nations and other bodies
found impossible to develop. For the church's understanding of
the theory or foundation of human rights to evolve has required
careful theological and magisterial work on several other fronts: a
theology of freedom, freedom of conscience, religious freedom,
political freedom, and a developmental understanding of moral
personality. The theory of human rights as finally developed by

the church is rooted in the natural law. The significance of this is that the church's theory of human rights could be potentially subscribed to universally since it is not tied to Catholic doctrinal positions. Briefly, this means that rights go with the turf of being a human being. They are God-given and "inalienable," and by carefully observing them one is obeying one's nature and the moral order with which it is scripted. Right reason about others' claims and needs as well as our own enables us to attain a flourishing human community. Moral thinking done from a natural law basis uncovers an objective moral order that, when observed, can make for harmony among peoples. If a claim to a right is legitimate (not all are, as we shall see), responding to the claim is a moral act. Perception of the dimensions of rights, their depth and breadth, and their inseparability from our responsibilities to one another is slowly dawning on the church, the faiths, and the nations.

Apart from natural law there will probably never be a more universally accepted theory or foundation for rooting human rights morally. Obviously, disputes about what rights are and aren't need something beyond the claims to determine which of the plaintiffs or positions is right and which wrong. Without an agreed-upon foundation, the asserted rights themselves are frequently contentious. In the matter of abortion, for example, pro-choice and pro-life are contradictory positions both voiced in terms of rights. There is an urgency about determining the theory that undergirds rights claims because without a theoretical warrant, rights easily become either cheap talk or a source of conflict. Either of these evoke hostility or indifference in a growing number of people of good will, with the result that modern civilizations could well lose the only moral category they had once agreed upon as legitimate.

The promise of human rights for generating harmony among peoples is unlimited if right reason, rather than vested or interested reason, is exercised by citizens, communities, and nations. The biggest impediment to right reason is reason dulled by deep individualism, which makes many citizens quick to claim rights but slow to take responsibilities. Responsibility for one another has to be the other half of a rights morality. The position of Pope John XXIII is that

> in human society, to one man's [*sic*] right there corresponds a duty in all other persons . . . for every fundamental human right draws its indestructible moral force from the natural law, which in granting it [a right] imposes a corresponding obligation . . . those who claim their own rights, yet forget or neglect to carry out their respective duties, are people who build with one hand and destroy with the other.[2]

The great value of a natural-law approach to understanding human rights is its universality. Where "human nature" exists, right reason can be operative. The nonvalue of rooting rights in the natural law is that the particular community, in this case the Roman Catholic community, isn't clear on how protecting, promoting, and observing rights is intrinsic to their faith. This is why holiness and rights are, for the most part, unconnected in the minds of Catholics. Rights are part of a generic morality, one all people of goodwill should be able to subscribe to. But for Catholics, many other Christians, and people of faith, they do not elicit the same response that teachings explicitly connected with Scripture and church doctrines do.

Viewing Human Rights Theologically

What I will do here is suggest some of the ways that Catholic Christians who take the call to holiness seriously could develop a theological understanding for incorporating human rights into their faith. The holiness they have received, and are called to abide in, would seem to require this attempt at integration. Rather than review the natural-law foundation that the church's teaching gives to human rights, I will suggest some theological themes we could enlist that closely connect our faith to human rights. Since these themes are more familiar, they should be able to elicit more of the affectivity helpful for the day-to-day living of the faith than natural-law reasoning.

CREATION/REDEMPTION

The infinite value of any human being in God's eyes should be obvious if we truly believe that each was made in God's own image and likeness. Each human was meant to live for eternity with humanity's Creator. Each human earthling was born with an immortality, and each is meant to hear a call to a destiny of union with the Triune God. The humanity of each person is the medium in which God's own justifying holiness is communicated. Original sin, which is the absence of that intended holiness, darkens the mind and weakens the will. But the Son of God laid down his life to restore God's original intention about human holiness. God's will is for "everyone to be saved and to come to the knowledge of the truth" (1 Tim. 2:4). Creation and redemption, therefore, are the two primary evidences of how seriously God takes each human being. Our interactions with one another must take these two actions of God as cues to our relations with one another. As Archbishop Desmond Tutu puts it: treating persons with any less than the dignity with which God has imbued them is a blasphemous act or like "spitting in the face of God."[3]

God's intention works when people are in, or attempt to be in, right relationship with one another. To be justified in God's eyes is God's gift to human beings streaming from the Christ-event. But that justification is meant also to produce an intramundane, empirical justice in relations between people. It is God's own justice, won by Christ, that is available to human beings and enables their being in right relationship with one another. But what does all this mean for rights? It means that the explicit coming into consciousness of one another's dignity as explicated by human rights is not only a major breakthrough in human relations but is further evidence of the working out of the gift of justification in history.

ESCHATOLOGY

The deep nobility of human rights activity, whether by observance, defense, or promotion, should not be missed. To put this dignity in eschatological terms, it could be said that where God's will is done, there the kingdom has already come in some inchoate form. But God's will is done where action on behalf of the needs of neighbor or fellow citizen is taken in view of their human dignity. The kingdom or reign of God materializes within time and history. The kingdom is the fruit of justice done to neighbor, freedoms fought for or accorded, love given or offered, human rights acted on. The kingdom is the sovereignty of the holy. Whatever is done on behalf of others' needs extends this sovereignty in time. This sovereignty lives more in the activity of hope, of course, than of realization. Acts of observing human rights generate two kinds of hope. One of these is intramundane, hope for the world and for our developing a harmony with one another. The other hope is world-transcending, hope for the world to come, the definitive eschaton, the absolute future, the eternal kingdom. But where people enjoy a social condition of immunity from being violated or violently treated and, therefore, the opportunity to flourish in their humanity, there God is glorified and the reign of God can grow thirty-, sixty-, and a hundredfold.

Those whose beliefs expect the kingdom of God would be wise to see that the evolution of the world in the direction of the observance of human rights is an unparalleled moment in the world's transformation toward the kingdom of God. "Signs of the times" aren't likely to get any better than this one. This is not a development parallel to or alongside salvation history. No, the breakout in the mid-twentieth century of sensitivity to the inviolable rights of human beings simply because of their humanity is intrinsic to salvation history. God is no less the author of human history than of salvation history. The church has learned from the world in this matter of human rights. While the church learned a rights morality from the world, it remains to be seen whether the secular world is willing to learn a rationale for its rights morality from the church. The church does not buy the whole rights package the world has. It critiques rights' claims from the aforesaid position of natural-law reasoning.

Lifting human rights to the level of association with the kingdom of God requires an academic distinction on the destiny of humanity in Christ. Eschatology views the present as able to flower into a future. It seeks an augur of a definitive future of justice and peace in the present. It thereby valorizes the efforts made in the course of history to bring about a world in which human rights are promoted, protected, and assiduously observed. Apocalyptic, by contrast, doesn't know what to make of the present or of history. Human efforts to bring about a just and peaceful world are hopscotched over in an effort to develop an ahistorical source of meaning. With eschatology, by contrast, the eternal future emerges from the history of what is intrinsic to every present. Christian eschatology expects that what humans have done in their pursuit of the true and the good, justice and peace, and human rights, will be brought into and recomposed in the final consummation in the new heavens and new earth. In this it is distinct from apocalyptic's belief that all this human effort will be left behind by a destructive conflagration of all that went before.

The Gospels

Reading the Gospel as a document that is actually promoting human dignity, even human rights, is an interesting and useful exercise. Jesus, the defender of human dignity par excellence, can be understood as exercising his ministry in terms of rights. The ministry of human rights could be greatly energized if Jesus' ministry were seen to be one in which the captives won their right to have a voice, the poor were given a new chance at economic viability, the blind won their sight by truth being told to them, and prisoners were rehabilitated to take their place in society with dignity. All of these are referred to in Jesus' mission statement, which he takes directly from Isaiah (Luke 4:18ff.).

It seems to me also that the Beatitudes and human rights have much in common. So much, in fact, that human rights might be seen as the modern beatitudes. Blessed are they who give and defend the right to life; they shall know the joy of it now and for all eternity. Blessed are those who are vindicated in standing up for their own and others' rights; they will know the consolation of God and of personal inviolability. Blessed are they who enjoy, and ensure for others, the privilege of an education; they will be Godlike in their ability to know the true and choose the good. Blessed are they who heal the sick or who fight to keep them from suffering without insurance coverage; they will know a flourishing that goes beyond time despite their own mortality. Blessed are they whose lives are lived on behalf of others; they will be counted among those who shall see God. In general, to fight for an immunity from violations to oneself and to one's community, is to be blessed.

SAINTS

The present pope, John Paul II, has beatified more *beati* and canonized more *sancti* than any previous pope in the history of the church. As I mentioned in the first chapter, there are two ways of looking at this proliferation. The one is that the *virtuosi* are becoming more numerous or are becoming more acknowledged. Wonderful as "their manifestation of the spirit" has been, they are still singular, leaving holiness seeming to be a race few have entered and even fewer have won. Another way of looking at this is that singling out the rare, one can easily miss the holiness of the communities that fomented their exceptionality. Even more unfortunate, it can also miss the fact of the holiness of the many and of the church itself in each of its communities.

But aside from all this, it seems to me that an invaluable study could be done about those whom the church has singled out for beatification and canonization. What was their relationship to human rights? Did their heroic virtue involve laying down their lives to address the legitimate claims of others for their material sustenance when they could not supply it for themselves? Did it involve fighting for the freedom of people to be self-determining when the political circumstances of their lives constrained or denied these rights? Did it involve laying down their lives so that communities could preserve the way of life these communities had known for aeons, even centuries in some cases? There are three generations of rights, according to the literature on rights. The first came out of the eighteenth century—civil and political rights. The second came out of the nineteenth century—social and economic rights. The third came out of the twentieth century—cultural and indigenous rights. It would be very helpful for the future of human rights if the church singled out greatness in terms of these kinds of rights. A saint has always been taken to be an embodiment of an ideal way for the rest of us to aspire to live our lives. Is there any reason why there couldn't be an explicit alignment of those, who in the past, at present, and in the future, embody holiness as those who have given their lives defending and promoting the rights of people?

A Deeper Scrutiny

To live a holy life that extends to, and includes, the political dimension requires one to be wise as a serpent and simple as a dove. Wisdom about rights is difficult to achieve and is only beginning to be achieved. I believe that theology can contribute somewhat to that wisdom. The insight into the Old Testament God as the One who could be disturbed into action on behalf of a violated people is germane here. God is still intimately involved in the protest being voiced by the violated. God disturbs us by every protest that comes to us from a human being whose well-being as human is under attack:

> The struggles for and claims about human rights are to be understood and interpreted as protests about something wrong or dehumanizing. Every time God comes across a situation of imbalance, deprivation, injustice, he is prepared to attack it, even if it means destroying Jerusalem.[4]

The protest itself voiced by human beings is the signal that a "divine attack" has begun on what is diminishing human dignity at a given point in time. Human rights would become much more central to a religious peoples' morality if they heard the protest of violation coming from God and not only from the violated.

All the faiths have everything to gain by taking rights into the center of their stories, their metanarratives. That would ensure their footing in reality as their faithful view it. By being rooted in the concrete circumstances of human diminishment, a faith changes from one that is overly concerned with itself and its growth and maybe even the growth of its constituents in union with God, to one that is concerned with what God seems concerned with here and now, the degrading of human dignity anywhere and everywhere that it occurs. *Gloria Dei vivens homo!* This is not an exhortation to naïveté. We can discern the difference between the voices of protest that resonate with the anger of God, calling for our response, and the voices of protest of people who haven't taken responsibility for their own well-being or who have come to some false understanding of rights.

But all faiths and their faithful also need to critique the extant rights morality. They need to see when it is being exploited by the selectively interested or by those who have twisted the understanding of human rights out of its natural law métier and created a rationale for them that is self-interested and therefore contrary to human flourishing. In particular I want to spell out here briefly what I mean by this. There has been a proliferation of ersatz rights by a judiciary that is culturally positivist in its jurisprudence. *Jurisimprudence,* to coin a term, answers only to laws and not to the higher law or to an objective order of morality. Rights morality is in serious need of the critique the faiths can bring to it. Without this critique, the idea of connecting holiness and rights will come to naught and can even become window dressing for unjustifiable rights claims.

Legal positivism is a species of a deeper confusion than taking law to be its own law. That deeper confusion is nominalism. It seems to me that the most serious criticism that can be leveled at a rights morality by any faith or philosophy is its penchant for nominalism. Just because something is called a right doesn't make it one. Like other forms of nominalism, the act of naming is the only reality the thing named has. Once there isn't anything about the objective order of morality that warrants the name of a right other than the convention that wants to call a particular claim a right, a rights morality soon becomes a matter of convention. So, if a mother carrying a fetus, for example, says that she has a right to choose whether the fetus will live, she has created a right for herself. The warrant she has for her right to choose, of course, comes from convention and from her government once it decided to legalize convention.

The Supreme Court has created a right, which in turn has spawned a number of new rights. The new right it created was the "right to privacy." It was born in 1965 when the Supreme Court in *Griswold v. Connecticut* claimed that such a right is embodied in our Constitution. This case has been subsequently ridiculed by many legal scholars because the Court never explained what exactly the "right to privacy" is or what it protects. But once this "right" was named, it began to take on a life of its own and spawned other rights.[5] In *Roe v. Wade* in 1973, the Court used this unexplained right and by regarding the fetus as not a person, developed another right: to abort the pregnancy. So both mother and Court can now act nominalistically. Neither of them has to acknowledge that there is a violation of the objective moral order by such an act. Instead we have the subjective preference of the mother to name her baby a fetus and, in effect, make herself a sovereign who can forfeit its life, and we have a rights-generating Court that has emboldened her choice about the baby's death and legalized her preference. If the Court had concluded that the fetus was human life as declared in the Constitution, then the fetus would have had the right to life and liberty. That would have made each abortion illegal, in fact a crime.

In 1992 with *Planned Parenthood v. Casey,* this line of reasoning reached its apogee. It spawned what has been called a mega-right when it pronounced: "At the heart of liberty is the right to define one's own concept of existence, of meaning, of the universe, and of the mystery of human life." This line of reasoning might be expected from a college sophomore, but it is difficult to believe that the Supreme Court would have let this preposterous mega-right see the light of day. Predictably, this dictum has been subsequently used to generate still another right, the right to die (in the 9th Circuit Court of Appeals on March 6, 1996, in *Compassion in Dying v. Washington*).

I cite these cases as a reminder that rights talk of itself must make one circumspect, or wise as a serpent and simple as a dove, because it is not always morally authentic and can be an exercise in wrong reason. I do not mean to demonize the Supreme Court here but only to underscore the need to be critical of some of its pronouncements on the subject of human rights. The moral order is not always in sync with the legal order, something that has been known since time immemorial. For a right to attain the status of a law is not necessarily evidence of the maturation of a right that should influence the faiths and their faithful, since it could be an invented counterfeit right, as the citations above indicate.

All of this material about rights can seem to be a distraction from the issue of holiness. It is only a seeming distraction, however. We cannot become or remain a holy people with our heads in the sand or by inhabiting some kind of apolitical stockade. The complexities about rights I cite here are not unknown to the majority of ordinary citizens, all of whom are called to holiness whether they know it or not. That call can issue in part from the political or outer rim of our connections with one another. Like the call that comes from our most intimate relationships, this call to political holiness must be heard and discerned. We must find God in all things, not only in those things already named "of God."

Eucharist

It seems to me, too, that Eucharist could be easily enlisted to shape the mind and heart about rights. The very first mention of the conduct of assemblies of worship in the New Testament (1 Cor. 11:17–34) is an account that upbraids the participants for their treatment of some of their fellow participants. The picture Paul paints is one of each clan taking care of itself, stuffing themselves and sometimes even having too much to drink. Rather than having a sense of the sacredness of each member of the assembly, some are left out of the sharing, even though those very same worshipers have a keen sense of the sacredness of the bread and the cup. But, Paul warns them: "Anyone who eats and drinks [the sacred species] without discerning the body [those gathered for worship], eats and drinks judgment on himself" (1 Cor. 11:29). Paul stings the Corinthians with the indictment that they are not eating the Lord's Supper but, by their allowing some of their fellow worshipers to go hungry, they have desacralized the supper. This disregard for another's need while taking care of oneself and one's own, profanes the spirituality of Eucharist. Recall that the Eucharist, at that time, was circumscribed by an *agapē* meal with all the elements of a hearty meal amply supplied by the participants. In effect, their denial of a place at the table for the misfits, rendered the assembly's rites so unworthy, it would have been better had they not been celebrated, Paul clearly says (1 Cor. 11:17).[6]

Why would he judge the Corinthians so harshly? Because we can presume that he knew what John knew, namely, "[This] bread . . . is my flesh for the life of the world" (John 6:51). The scope of the eucharistic participants had to widen to include those their culture had taught them to exclude. They had to learn that the point of the Eucharist was not simply their own spiritual nurture; it was nothing short of the life of the whole community and, beyond it, the world.

What the Giver of the gift of Eucharist is concerned about is enhancing the dignity of each person who has been given life by God, each to increase "the praise of his Glory." The life of the world is abstract; the life of persons is concrete. What is Eucharist given for? Not simply the life of union between the recipient and God, but communion between the recipient and the congregation and the life of the world beyond the congregation. But the life of the world beyond the congregation can be concretely understood in terms of the human rights of all the citizens of the world.

In the previous chapter we have looked at solidarity and holiness. Solidarity, like any virtue, needs a repeated action to become habitual. And it needs a story from which it is acted out. For Christians, solidarity has such an action and story. It is Eucharist. That is where the story is best learned and the virtue exercised and "a firm determination to commit oneself to the common good" made. Eucharist is where "doing your own thing" is transcended. Eucharist "done" is training in, and an experience of, solidarity. What could have more solidarity than a community of people who know that they are in Christ, that in him they have died, and that their lives are meaningful because of him in whom they have learned to live and move and have their being as one?

Eucharist is an action of a people that fashions the people who do it into one bread broken for others and one cup poured out for the life of the world. Eucharist is both received as gift and done as a firm determination to replicate the self-donating act of the One the sacrament commemorates. Eucharist is a call to solidarity and the conferral of the energy for the work of solidarity. Eucharist is a local and a cosmic action where the fruits of the earth are transformed through the power of the Holy Spirit and the words of institution into an augur of the future, transfigured world. Eucharist is where the public is transformed into a commons and a common good is made, distributed, and received.

The epicenter of the common good at its uncommon best is the christological good where many are made one at a given moment of time and space. What is both common and uncommonly good about this is that because of Eucharist the participants are membered one to another. They are now who he is and he is who they are. How could there be a greater solidarity than this? From this moment and from this conferral of energy there is to come forth a change in the possibility for the common good beyond Eucharist. "[This] bread . . . is my flesh for the life of the world," the life, that is, of a community confecting and effecting the common good.

Eucharist can also be a failure in solidarity as Corinth was. A failed Eucharist truncates the Christ-event, and some portion of the world is deprived of the life it was meant to know and the common meaning it was meant to enjoy. In the coming together for Eucharist, the body was not discerned, the body material, the body Christic, the body ecclesial, the body politic. Rather than a prayer emitted from the lips of the concelebrants, some antisolidarity sentiment is being expressed similar to that of the great theologian Jimmy Durante: "Why doesn't everyone just leave everyone else the hell alone?"

One of the deepest deprivations of a failed Eucharist is that it has ever widening ramifications: Christ is not known by the world through the solidarity of the concelebrants, but even by the concelebrants themselves. He remains imaged as singular rather than as he truly is now, many-membered and present in the community made one in him in the Spirit. As a church, we have spent much time trying to understand the metaphysical constitution of Christ both in his historical life and in his risen life. Precious little time has been spent understanding what has happened to him now that he has risen. It is not only we who change by being in Christ. He has changed by being in us. We change him. Our flesh changes him into bread for the life of the world.

Postscript

THIS MORNING I PICKED UP a document that has been lying on my to-be-read pile for several months. It is Pope John Paul II's Apostolic Letter in which he reflects on our entry into the new millennium. By means of the symbol of the holy door that he closes with the ending of the Jubilee year he exhorts us "to leave more fully open the living door which is Christ."[1] Because of what he highlights in this letter, I feel elated and confirmed in the choice of themes I have made in writing this book. The things that he is sure all of us must attend to in this new millennium are the following: the gift and task of holiness, a spirituality of communion, human rights, the Eucharist, and the glory of God. The best summary I can give to the whole book is to put it in the terms used in this remarkable document.

First of all, his letter echoes what I tried to call attention to in the first chapter that "the objective gift of holiness is offered to all the baptized" (Ibid., 30). The pope here reminds us that this gift of holiness is "a universal call" that needs to be reheard. He also reminds us that holiness, according to the council, is "an

intrinsic and essential aspect of the teaching on the church" (Ibid.,
30). The church belongs to him "who is in essence the Holy One,
the thrice Holy" (cf. Isa. 6:3), whose sacrifice of himself was made
"precisely in order to make the bride of Christ holy" (Ibid., 30).
Not content to leave the matter of holiness to a gift we have
received, he declares it to be "a task which must shape the whole
of Christian life: 'This is the will of God, your holiness'" (1 Thess.
4:3) (Ibid., 30). Although we probably didn't know it at the time
of our baptisms, the letter comments that "baptism is a true entry
into the holiness of God through incorporation into Christ and
the indwelling of his Spirit." Since this is so, "it would be a contradiction to settle for a life of mediocrity marked by a minimalist
ethic and a shallow religiosity" (Ibid., 31).

Most welcome, too, is the pope's reminder, as I tried to
underscore in my text, that holiness "must not be misunderstood
as if it involved some kind of extraordinary existence, possible
only for a few uncommon heroes of holiness" (Ibid., 31). Equally
welcome is his mentioning that "this primacy of holiness and
prayer is inconceivable without a renewed listening to the word
of God" (Ibid., 39). I hope my second chapter, on the ways
in which holiness unfolds in the Hebrew Scriptures, and the
third chapter, on how Jesus' consciousness of his specialness
developed through the Word, helped to connect holiness, prayer,
and the word of God in the mind of the reader. I was happy, too,
that the pope parallels what I tried to stress in chapters 4 and 5,
that holiness must be connected to "the most ordinary circumstances of life," as these unfold in both our desires and our
pedestrian habits.

The pope then develops his oft-repeated theme of solidarity
into something he felicitously calls a "spirituality of communion."
He roots this spirituality in "the heart's contemplation of the mystery of the Trinity dwelling in us and whose light we must also be

able to see shining on the faces of the brothers and sisters around us . . . (thereby learning) how to make room for them and to bear each other's burdens" (Ibid., 43). In the last two chapters of my book, a spirituality of communion is exactly what I have been trying to articulate but did not have the wit to so name. He speaks of human rights in terms of seeing the face of Christ in the hungry, the thirsty, the stranger, the naked, the sick, the imprisoned since it was with these "that he himself wished to be identified" (Ibid., 49). "By these words [of Matt. 25:31 ff.] no less than by the orthodoxy of her doctrine, the church measures her fidelity as the bride of Christ" (Ibid., 49).

Never far from each part of his letter is this theme of the glory of God. He had announced the Jubilee itself as something he hoped "would be lived as one unceasing hymn of praise to the Trinity" since "the duty of praise is the point of departure for every genuine response of faith to the revelation of God in Christ" (Ibid., 4). He then launches into a paean of praise for the two thousand years in which sinners have needed mercy and have been met with the freshness of the "today of salvation." Fully aware that not only sinners but the church itself "is at once holy and always in need of being purified," he cannot withhold his "Glory to you, Jesus Christ, for you reign today and forever" (Ibid., 5).

Finally, throughout my text I have alluded to Eucharist, as does the pope. In particular, he connects it with solidarity and a spirituality of communion. "The Sunday eucharist, which every week gathers Christians together as God's family round the table of the word and the bread of life, is also the most natural antidote to dispersion. It is the privileged place where communion is ceaselessly proclaimed and nurtured. Precisely through sharing in the eucharist, the Lord's Day also becomes the day of the church, when she can effectively exercise her role as the sacrament of unity" (Ibid., 36).

The pope ends his letter on the note of stretching, of all things! The pilgrimage we have undertaken with the holy year (and with this book), "will have as it were stretched our legs for the journey still ahead. We need to imitate the zeal of Paul, who said, 'straining forward to what lies ahead, I press on toward the goal for the prize of the upward call of God in Jesus Christ'" (Phil. 3:13–14) (Ibid., 59).

Endnotes

Chapter 1

1. Quotations from council documents are from *Lumen Gentium, The Documents of Vatican II*, ed. Walter M. Abbott, S.J. (New York: Herder & Herder, 1966).

2. "By holiness a more human way of life is promoted" (*LG*, 40).

3. There is a variation in the translations of this line, many preferring "consecrated" to "sanctified"; for example, the New American Bible's translation reads ". . . he has made perfect forever those who are being consecrated."

4. In Pope John Paul II's first encyclical, *Redemptor Hominis*, he affirms, "Christ has redeemed every human person, without exception, because Christ is in a way united to every human person without exception, even if the individual does not recognize this fact."

5. A useful book on this process is David Peterson, *Possessed by God: A New Testament Theology of Sanctification and Holiness* (Grand Rapids, Mich.: Eerdmans, 1995), 35.

6. See Norbert Lohfink, S.J., *The Covenant Never Revoked: Biblical Reflections on Christian-Jewish Dialogue* (New York: Paulist Press, 1991).

7. See Kilian McDonnell, "Theological Presuppositions in Our Preaching about the Spirit," *Theological Studies* 59 (1998): 222.

8. Raniero Cantalamessa, *The Holy Spirit in the Life of Jesus: The Mystery of Christ's Baptism* (Collegeville, Minn.: Liturgical Press, 1994), 15.

9. Servais Pinckaers, O.P., "The Sermon on the Mount," chap. 6 in *The Sources of Christian Ethics*, trans. Sr. Mary Thomas Noble (Washington, D.C.: Catholic University of America Press, 1995), 251–78.

Chapter 2

1. I have found John G. Gammie's *Holiness in Israel* (Minneapolis, Minn.: Fortress Press, 1989) helpful in making these selections.

2. For an excellent introduction to the scholarship on the Pentateuch, see Joseph Blenkinsopp, *The Pentateuch*, in Anchor Bible Reference Library (New York: Doubleday, 1992).

3. Second Isaiah expresses this development vividly: "For he who has become your husband is your Maker; his name is the LORD of hosts;

Your redeemer is the Holy One of Israel, called God of all the earth" (Isa. 54:5).

4. Abraham Joshua Heschel, *The Sabbath: Its Meaning for Modern Man* (New York: Farrar, Straus & Giroux, 1995), 43.

5. Walter Bruggemann, *The Prophetic Imagination* (Philadelphia: Fortress Press, 1978).

6. "Chapter 31 constitutes a high-water mark in Old Testament ethics," according to John Gammie (*Holiness in Israel*, 146).

Chapter 3

1. Gerald O'Collins, S.J., and Daniel Kendall, S.J., review the growing literature on the subject of Jesus' faith including this point about the mistranslation of Hebrews ("The Faith of Jesus," in *Theological Studies* 53 [1992]: 403 ff.).

2. International Theological Commission, *Texts and Documents,* 1969–1985, ed. Michael Sharkey (San Francisco: Ignatius Press, 1989), 185–205, 206–23, 305–16.

3. Karl Rahner, "Dogmatic Reflections on the Knowledge and Self-Consciousness of Christ," in *Theological Investigations* 5 (Baltimore: Helicon Press, 1966), 193–215.

4. *Decrees of the Ecumenical Councils,* ed. Norman P. Tanner 1 (Washington, D.C.: Georgetown University Press, 1990) 86.

5. William V. Dych, *Thy Kingdom Come: Jesus and the Reign of God* (New York: Crossroad, 1999), 7.

6. Raniero Cantalamessa, *The Holy Spirit in the Life of Jesus* (Collegeville, Minn.: Liturgical Press, 1994), 5.

Chapter 4

1. I take all this story from Ignatius's own autobiography, which can be found in *St. Ignatius' Own Story: As Told to Luis González de Cámera*, trans. by William J. Young, S.J. (Chicago: Henry Regnery Company, 1956).

2. Peter Kreeft, ed., *A Summa of the Summa: The Essential Theological Passages of St. Thomas Aquinas' Summa Theologica*, I question 16, article 1 (San Francisco: Ignatius Press, 1990), 145.

3. Louis J. Puhl, S.J., trans. *The Spiritual Exercises of St. Ignatius* (Chicago: Loyola University Press, 1951), 12.

4. This quotation is taken from a letter Ignatius wrote to the Jesuits at Ferrara; it is quoted in the third volume of the twelve-volume *Monumenta Historica Societatis Jesu*. It has been translated by William J. Young, S.J., in his *Letters of St. Ignatius of Loyola* (Chicago: Loyola University Press, 1959), 245.

5. E. Edward Kinert, "Eliciting Great Desires," *Studies in the Spirituality of Jesuits* 16 (November 1984): 16. This whole issue is excellent on desires in Ignatius.

Chapter 5

1. Gregory of Nyssa is quoted by David Granfield, *Heightened Consciousness: The Mystical Differences* (New York: Paulist Press, 1991), 176.

2. Bonaventure, *The Mind's Road to God,* trans. George Boas (New York: Liberal Arts Press, 1953), 12.

3. Bernard J. F. Lonergan, *Method in Theology* (New York: Herder & Herder, 1972), 106.

4. Anders Nygren, *Agape and Eros,* trans. Philip S. Watson (Philadelphia: Westminster, 1953).

5. Louis J. Puhl, S.J., trans. "Introduction to Making a Choice of a Way of Life," in *The Spiritual Exercises of St. Ignatius* (Chicago: Loyola University Press, 1951), 169.

6. Hans Urs von Balthasar, *Two Sisters in the Spirit: Thérése of Lisieux and Elizabeth of the Trinity* (San Francisco: Ignatius Press, 1992), 20. (All quotations in this section are taken from this volume.)

Chapter 6

1. John Paul II, *Sollicitudo Rei Socialis* 40. See *Catholic Social Thought: The Documentary Heritage,* ed. David J. O'Brien and Thomas A. Shannon (Maryknoll, N.Y.: Orbis Books, 1992), 423.

2. Jane Blewett, "The Greening of Catholic Social Thought," *Pro Mundi Vita Studies* (February 1990): 29.

3. Elizabeth A. Johnson, "Discerning Kinship with Earth," in *Women, Earth and Creator Spirit* (New York: Paulist Press, 1993), 31.

4. Thomas Berry, *The Dream of the Earth* (San Francisco: Sierra Club Books, 1988).

5. Karl Rahner, *Hominization: The Evolutionary Origin of Man as a Theological Problem*, trans. W. I. O'Hara (New York: Herder & Herder, 1965), 19.

6. Karl Rahner, "The Unity of Spirit and Matter in the Christian Understanding of Faith," in *Theological Investigations*, 6:108.

7. Michael W. Petty, *A Faith That Loves the Earth: The Ecological Theology of Karl Rahner* (Lanham, Md.: University Press of America, 1996), 182–83. (This volume has been very helpful for this whole section.)

8. Karl Rahner, "Christology within an Evolutionary View of the World," in *Theological Investigations*, 5:176.

9. Karl Rahner, "The Resurrection of the Body," in *Theological Investigations*, 2:213.

10. For example, John Paul II, *Sources of Renewal: The Implementation of the Second Vatican Council* (San Francisco: Harper & Row, 1980), 121.

11. "Final Report of Extraordinary Synod of 1985," *Origins* (December 19, 1985): 448.

Chapter 7

1. See John C. Haughey, S.J., "Vienna Diary: Moving from Wrongs to Rights," *The Woodstock Report* 35 (October 1993): 4.

2. *Pacem in Terris* 30, quoted in *Catholic Social Thought: The Documentary Heritage,* ed. David J. O'Brien and Thomas A. Shannon (Maryknoll, N.Y.: Orbis Books, 1992), 135.

3. Desmond Tutu, "Reflections by a Nobel Laureate," in *The Universal Declaration of Human Rights: Fifty Years and Beyond,* ed. Yael Danieli, Elsa Stamatopoulou, and Clarence J. Dias (Amityville, N.Y.: Baywood, 1999), xiii.

4. David Jenkins, "Theological Enquiry Concerning Human Rights," *Ecumenical Review* 2 (April 1975): 99.

5. Mary Ann Glendon, *Rights Talk: The Impoverishment of Political Discourse* (New York: Free Press, 1991), 57–61.

6. John C. Haughey, S.J., "Eucharist at Corinth: You Are the Christ," in *Above Every Name: The Lordship of Christ and Social Systems,* ed. Thomas E. Clarke (Ramsey, N.J.: Paulist Press, 1980), 107–33.

Postscript

1. John Paul II, "Apostolic Letter *Novo Millennio Ineunte*," *Origins* 30 (January 18, 2001): Introduction.

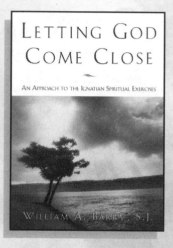